The step-by-step guide to
success in the music

JM

Brea

or Young
Bands

by ED Berman.

Omnibus Press/Inter-Action In-Print

Written, designed and produced by
Inter-Action Social Enterprise Trust.
Edited by ED Berman.
Production Managers Bob Chase & Peter Mount.
Book designed by Barry Child.
Cover designed by Pearce Marchbank.
Photographs by Roland Kemp, Jon Blackmore, Pete Anderson,
Blackfriars Settlement, Bob Chase, Adrian Neville.
Typsetting by Rowland Phototypesetting (London) Ltd.

The publishers are grateful to the following
for their help in the preparation of this book:
Audio Services; The Basement Project; Dave Bedford;
Martin Goldschmidt; The Gateshead Music Collective;
The Islington Arts Factory; Erica Lander;
The Lewisham Academy of Music; MCPS;
The Musicians Union; Professional Percussion;
The Riverside Music Co-op; Cuthbert Richards; Save & Prosper;
The Simionics; Sutton and Winson; Claudia Stumpfl;
The Tudor Trust; The Wates Foundation; Zomba Records.

Exclusive Distributors:
Book Sales Limited,
8/9 Frith Street, London W1V 5TZ, England.
Music Sales Corporation,
24 East 22nd Street,
New York NY 10010, USA.
Music Sales Pty. Limited,
120 Rothschild Avenue, Rosebery, NSW 2018, Australia.
To the Music Trade only:
Music Sales Limited,
8/9 Frith Street, London W1V 5TZ.

Order No. OP 43926
ISBN 0.7119.0978.4

Contents

Continued

28th May, 1984

Dear ED,

It strikes me that you brought this book out too late. If only I had this information when I set out to be a musician, it would have been much easier.

You see I tended to learn by my mistakes, very expensive ones. The great thing about the music industry is that it's one of the few fields left where you can actually do most things yourself. It's a real life adventure where there aren't really any limits.

However, as in most things, getting started is the most difficult and the most dangerous, and it's quite easy to get lost in the morass of publishing deals, recording deals, contracts, rip off merchants, managers, etc... where young talent is strangled at birth rather than carefully nurtured as it should be. I know of no nobler occupation than to call oneself a musician, and Britain has for some inexplicable reason produced a disproportionate number of bands and musicians. In commercial terms, there is no more dynamic or exciting growth industry as music, so I consider it of the upmost importance that young talent wherever it might be is given the best opportunity possible to express itself.

This book provides a blueprint for survival and a handbook to the school of hard knocks that is show business, and is worthy of attention from all musicians, regardless of experience or ability. Music is for all.

Sting

Foreword

IS MUSIC MONEY TO YOUR EARS? by ED Berman

Most people think that the main problem facing talented young bands today is money - or the lack of it. I used to think the same way until I met a young bands' collective in the North. They asked me to do a workshop with them on how to organize their own Centre, to be run by local young people themselves.

Amazingly, they didn't want to talk about raising money to do it – they already had a huge grant – over £100,000. Their problem was that they couldn't spend it! They didn't know how to get hold of a building, nor how to set up an organization.

It wasn't entirely their fault: you can't blame young people for not having experience. Everyone has to start somewhere. But that group of young people got me thinking that all young bands must face the same problems when starting out – getting rehearsal space, getting equipment and getting organized.

Our school system doesn't let young people find out how to do these things themselves – certainly not as a group or team. And there isn't a book that gives the practical information they need. Not that you can learn experience from a handbook; but at least you can learn the rules of the game, where to get advice and how to start.

There can't be a band in the country which hasn't had problems getting rehearsal space and equipment at some time or other. I had worked with many young bands in the recording studio at the Inter-Action Centre. Also I had worked around the country on a project called MIY – Make-It-Yourself: with the help of their own youth workers, many different groups of young people made and sold their own singles and albums.

All of this led me to think that the idea of a shared music space – a 'Breaks Centre' for many bands – was both needed and very possible for young people to do any-

where. Ideally this is best done with the help of a local youth worker or business adviser: but even they would need an outline to follow.

Although *Breaks for Young Bands* is only the sub-title of this book, I have used it throughout when referring to the book itself. *Breaks for Young Bands* isn't about making big money out of music – and most young bands know that's a fantasy anyway. *Breaks for Young Bands* is about having fun and learning new skills. It's about how to get organized and how to work together in a group. Even if you don't end up earning a living through music, these skills are useful in anything you do.

Everyone knows that the hype surrounding the few bands who have 'made it' in the media sense is only the tip of an iceberg. There's lots of hard work and dedication by tens of thousands of young bands out there – and often they don't get the help they should. Why is it that young musicians get so little help from rock stars? Given the problems that everyone in our society faces today, pop stars do owe something, if only to pass on their experience to others.

When I compare the general picture in the pop world to what's happening in the business world, the difference is amazing. More and more business people are giving time to help young people set up their own businesses including 'Breaks Centres'. That's why you'll find lots of business organizations to go to for help listed in this book. However, there's not even one helpful address backed by a rock star.

Of course, rock stars and big name groups get sackloads of letters asking for help everyday. They don't have time to sort out the cons from the genuine good proposals. So why don't they set up charitable trusts to get this pressure off their backs? All requests for help could be dealt with by a Trust acting under guidelines from the donors. Funds could be put back efficiently into the community in a variety of well-planned ways.

The Band Aid phenomenon is not the sort of thing I'm talking about, even though it was amazing, useful and necessary. What I am talking about is a large number of smaller regular efforts by those who have 'made it'. These would help grass roots projects which their fans and any other young person might constructively participate in.

I asked Sting to write the Intro to this book because I know he has put some of his spare time and money where his mouth is – helping up-and-coming young bands – through a Trust he set up. Although Sting is not the only one, it's a pity that many more stars – who make money out of young people and out of the themes of love, peace and righting the wrongs of the world – don't practice what they preach.

There's always going to be an element of luck in making it as a young band – and there's no substitute for basic music sense and hard work. But there are lots of things you can do for yourself to improve your own deal. This book is a down-to-earth guide to setting about making your own break and learning skills that can be used anywhere.

Preface

GETTING STUCK IN

Breaks For Young Bands (remember we're using the sub-title to refer to this book) is an introduction to getting into popular music - from choosing and learning to play an instrument, starting a band, rehearsing and gigging - to creating a Breaks Centre for young bands to share rehearsal space, lessons, advice and equipment.

This book is a step-by-step guide. So the first part is for the beginner and deals with the basics: getting equipment and learning to play. The rest of Part One deals with setting up a band and how to get a variety of breaks for it.

Part Two is for young people who want to go further. This future stage would be to help themselves and other young musicians in their area by setting up a Breaks For Young Bands Centre. In such a Centre, resources and facilities can be shared.

If you're only interested in deals and contracts, or starting up a Breaks Centre, or some other specific topic, then of course you can use the Contents List to turn straight to that part. Even if you're quite experienced though, you might pick up some tips by reading it right through, starting with the beginners' bits on the first few pages.

There's a lot of learning to be done before you can play music that sounds both good and confident. If you've never tried, here are a couple of things to think about.

Do you have a sense of rhythm – can you keep time with a record? Can you sing in tune? Even if you don't see yourself as a vocalist, it's a great help. If someone plays two different notes on an instrument, can you definitely hear the difference between one note and another? And can you sing these two notes in tune after they've been played to you?

Without being able to do these simple things you'll probably find it difficult to master an instrument. But then, you never know until you try. Even if you know you're not cut out to be the next Boy George, there are lots of other ways for you to become involved in music.

Bands need people to take care of equipment, design posters, do sound mixing and so forth. They often need managers.

You could also help to organize a Breaks For Young Bands Centre – everything from technical help to fund-raising will be needed. If you want to set up a Breaks Centre, your best bet is to speak first to local youth or community workers. They may know of a secure space in a building which will have people around who have your interests at heart.

PART ONE

A START FOR YOURSELF
A BREAK FOR YOUR BAND

Equipment

To make sure you get the right equipment you're going to need a lot of advice. You probably have an idea of what instrument you want to play. More often than not you'll be attracted to the sound of the instrument. If you can, you should have a go on one before buying anything. Even if you can't play anything on it, you'll get an idea of what it feels like. Try to understand how it works. If you go to either a youth centre or college you might find people there on a music course who could help you.

It's a good idea at this stage to build up a relationship with a band who play regularly in your area. Find one whose music you enjoy. Go to see them as often as you can. They'll recognize you and appreciate your coming to swell their audience. Without bothering them when they're busy, tell them what you want to do and ask if you can meet them sometime to get their advice.

Be serious. Ask them how they get certain sounds, whey they chose a certain piece of equipment, what it does and how it works.

Be gentle but persistent. They'll realize how much you want to have a go. They might invite you along to one of their rehearsals and give you a chance to "mess around" with the stuff. If there's something you don't know, then ask. To repay their favour it might be possible for you to help them in some way. Perhaps you can help them pack the gear off stage, distribute leaflets, or do some posters for them.

By being with more experienced people you'll learn about the kind of equipment you're going to need. Why make your own costly mistakes when you can learn from others who've made and paid for them already?

Another useful thing to do is to visit your local music shop. Tell them what you're interested in. Someone is likely to demonstrate and explain it to you. Once again, be very serious about it. Don't just lark around. Sadly, these days if young people invade a shop, the staff assume you're out to

waste their time – or worse, to pinch something.

Tell them how badly you want to learn. That way they're likely to treat you as a potential future customer. Every shop needs these. Even so, don't hang around there every day. Remember to get an idea of the prices of the things you want.

Hopefully you'll now have a list of 'bare essentials' – the basic ingredients of a band. Your musician friends will be able to help you make sure you've decided on the right stuff. Then you can look through the columns in the music papers for second-hand gear. Papers like *NME* or *Melody Maker* are especially useful. You really must get someone else's help here. The chances of your getting exactly what you need the first time are small without good advice from someone with experience.

Certain bits of equipment will only work when you have expensive 'extras'. For example, it's no use deciding to buy a fantastic microphone only to find later that you'll need an expensive power supply unit to run it. Also, some equipment won't work with other equipment. They just can't be matched; this is because of impedances. An experienced band can explain this. You could also go to your local library and look it up.

At its simplest, each piece of equipment has an impedance rating. This is a number measured by an electrical term, 'ohms'. These numbers must match up. For example, if you wanted to couple two loudspeakers together, they should both have the same rating – whether it's 4 ohms, 8 ohms or 16 ohms.

Hopefully this book will be of use to you whatever type of music you want to play. Rock music, for example, still uses the basic format of drums, bass, and maybe two other guitars. Recent years have seen many different instruments added to that. Keyboards, stringed instruments like violins and cellos, and wind instruments like flutes, clarinets and saxophones are all now fairly standard.

But don't go by a standard line-up. You can play whatever instrument you want. If you learn to play it well there will always be a place for you. If it's an unusual instrument you may make a lot of difference to a band. You'll make them sound different from all the rest and they'll attract more attention.

You'll find our from the musicians that it's easier to go about buying some instruments than others. Here are a few hints though.

Guitars Generally, the better made a guitar is, the easier it is to play. Some of the cheaper ones are terrible. The 'action' is too high, which, put simply, means you have to press incredibly hard to get the strings down on to the fretboard or neck to play the chord. This will give you terrible dents in the fingertips of your left hand. If you carried on they would probably cut and bleed all over your 'nice' guitar and be very painful. By the way, your fingertips will in any case take time to get stronger, but it should be a fairly painless process.

Often the neck of a guitar is not angled onto the body properly. This makes it impossible to get correctly tuned notes all the way up the neck; but you need this if you're ever going to play guitar solos. They must always be

properly pitched – especially if you're going to play or sing with others. People will accuse you of being badly tuned or even of playing badly. That hurts more than cut fingers!

Synthesizers These have to be chosen carefully and looked after like the delicate electronic instruments they are – if you're lucky enough to be able to afford one in the first place. When buying second-hand remember that some of the older ones, if they break down, are useless. It might not be possible to find anyone who's got the spare parts for them. Get advice from a keyboard player. There's quite a lot to know about them. You'll probably need to be handy with a screwdriver some of the time.

15

Drums There aren't too many problems about buying a good second-hand drum kit. Just check whether the threads are worn at the top of the cymbal and tom-tom stands. If they are, the drums won't be held securely and you'll need to buy new stands. Also make sure the spur, which the bass sits on, holds it securely in place. If it doesn't do the job, your drum may try to join the London Marathon when you hit it.

For a basic kit you'll need a bass drum, a snare drum and a pair of hi-hat cymbals. These will give you all the sounds you'll need. It's also easier starting with just a few drums. Don't aim yet for the kind of kit you see bands using on TV. Wait until you can use a basic one first.

A second-hand kit will probably cost somewhere between £80 and £100; new it will cost between £200 and £300. For anything less than that you're unlikely to get a particularly good sound.

You're best off starting with a pair of medium weight drum-sticks. Once you've got the strength in your wrists, you can then progress to lighter or heavier sticks, according to your type of music.

It's not really a good idea to start off learning about percussion with the aid of a drum machine. You still need a good sense of rhythm to be able to use them properly, and this is best learned on a real kit. They're also expensive and less flexible, making them of little use to a reggae band, for example.

Value for Money At this stage you should be looking for the best instrument it's possible to get for your budget. A very good instrument is a very good investment. If you simply buy the first one you see, it's likely to be worthless in a few months' time. Look at the brand name. Maybe you'll have seen that name a lot in adverts in musicians' papers.

Some guitars, like Fenders or Gibsons, are very expensive. But they have been making them for a long time, so you may find a very old one for a reasonable price. You might even, accidentally, get one of the older ones that are much sought after and can fetch more money than the brand new ones!

You've got to be extremely careful about second-hand stuff. The people selling it to you have no legal obligations for the thing to be in perfect working order. It might be useless. Use your common sense. Make sure you know that the things you buy are the right ones for you – that they work properly, that there are people around who can repair them, and that there's someone who stocks the spare parts which might need replacing.

If you're certain of these things and you've taken advice, then offer the sellers a bit less than they asked in the advert. Haggle. They might not like seeing you walk away without it – they want the money and probably pretty badly.

Apart from adverts in the music papers or shop windows, another way of buying good cheap gear is by asking other musicians. Often they'll have changed the type of music they're playing, so some gear won't be needed anymore. If not, they may know other bands who have surplus equipment. It's even better if you already know these people. Then you'll know what the truth is likely to be. Also you'll get more valuable advice on how to squeeze the best use out of it.

Ask them about any extras that might be needed. The gear might need special leads or pedals or stands which could prove to be an extra expense. You could ask them if they're still using them. If not, you might even get them thrown in free – or for a couple of quid. At least ask. Asking is the only thing that doesn't cost anything!

When getting any piece of equipment, try, if you can, to get a case for it. Sometimes it will be an aluminium flightcase. Obviously the case will protect the gear and save you repair costs.

Microphones If people in a band are going to sing or use acoustic instruments, they'll each need a microphone. There are hundreds of different types and they all have different uses. Some mikes are great with drum kits but lousy with vocals. With some it's the other way around.

However, certain microphones – such as those made by Unisound, Beyer, Shure or AKG – do the job very well and some models are reasonably cheap. They're in common use with most bands. These can generally be used to mike up all sorts of different instruments and still be used for vocals.

Be very careful about buying second-hand mikes unless you've tested them. If they've been dropped they can sound very odd. They may not pick up anything at all!

When you get a mike don't forget to get a stand for it – one that will reach the height you want and is easily adjustable. Because of the huge variety of mikes, you'll need to be able to screw on different 'clips' to the end of the stand to hold the particular mike you're using. Make sure the stand hasn't got a clip glued onto it. And make sure you get supplied with the correct clip. It should slide over your mike fairly easily and hold it snugly. Check with local bands as to which mikes they use and why.

Amplifiers If you're playing an electric guitar or bass, or using a microphone, you'll need an amplifier. This is a piece of electrical gear which takes the tiny current produced by a guitar or microphone and jacks it up to enough current to power a loudspeaker.

The best sort of amplifier to start off with is probably a 'combo' – an amplifier combined with a speaker in one unit. For practising and playing in a small band, an amp of about 50 watts power will be enough. The higher the number of watts, the louder the volume output.

Make sure you get someone who knows about amps to play an instrument through the one you're thinking of buying. Listen to its tone. Make sure it doesn't distort the sound. Check that all the switches and knobs work properly before you decide to spend your money.

Other Bands If you're already formed into what will one day be a band, check out how any other newly started bands in your area are going. Keep in touch all the time. You're not really competitors. You can learn from each other. You can help each other too, either by loaning equipment if it's not being used, or by hiring it out cheaply. Before you hand over anything though, make sure you come to some arrangement in case things go wrong with the gear. Decide who will pay for it to be repaired.

Hire-Purchase It is possible to buy equipment on hire-purchase (HP). This is simply when you buy something by paying for it in instalments – small, regular payments.

It might sound like the ideal solution. There are problems though. Companies charge interest to let you do that. The average rate at the moment is about 30 per cent. So for every hundred pounds' worth of stuff you buy on HP, you're really having to pay £130. You will also have to be over twenty-one and have a job that pays a steady wage.

Think about it carefully. It does mean you can get gear quickly without having to wait until you've saved; but it will cost you a lot more.

Safety If you're buying an electric instrument (guitar,

bass, etc.) or an amplifier, microphone or synthesizer, make sure you check its electrical safety. If there's something wrong with the wiring (for example, if it's not earthed), you may well get a shock off it. If you've ever experienced the shock of a live microphone against your teeth, you'll probably be careful enough in future. In order to avoid this shocking dentistry, it's best by far to take precautions from the start.

If your equipment isn't earthed, you can charge up everything metal in the room. This is a very easy way of starting a big fire. By and large, sound equipment isn't all that dangerous if you've wired it up properly, because it doesn't use all that much electricity. So it's vital you check that each piece of equipment and plug is properly wired. If you're not sure about wiring, then ask an electrician, or at least get a chart from a hardware shop and follow it.

When plugging the band's gear into the mains, never use more then one adaptor. It's much safer to use flat spreader boards which have four sockets in a line. Remember that electric fires and kettles must be run off a separate power point from the one the band is using.

Learning the Instrument

This is where you have to wave goodbye to a lot of your social life! There's no time to flop in front of the telly anymore. You must play and play to get familiar with the instrument. Hopefully you'll be so keen it won't seem like hard work.

You'll hear lots of stories about some musicians, even famous ones, who claim they never had a proper music lesson in their life. They say they were never properly taught how to play technically. It could be true, say, one in a million times. It really is advisable to take at least a few lessons from an experienced teacher. It is vitally important you get this kind of solid background – even perhaps learning how to read music.

You'll learn the basic keys and technique, like how to

move your fingers in the correct way. Without that you'll never develop the right strength in your hands to be able to play the instrument properly. Without basic technique you'll probably not be able to grow all that fast musically.

Check out the situation in your area. If you're unemployed you might get lessons for next to nothing. Check your local music teachers for this; also the adult education centre.

Learning with others is a good way. That way no one will dare 'bottle out'. You also have to practise a lot and it can be boring at first.

If you can get several other people together who also want to learn a musical instrument, you might persuade an adult education centre or a youth club to lay on a course for you.

At the same time as you're having these lessons you might be able to find one or two musicians willing to help you out. This can be very useful. Apart from being a constant source of encouragement because they play so well, they'll make you see the reasons for having the formal lessons. The next step is practice – so's the one after that!

Learning to play may seem difficult at first. But it should also be fun. Because you seem to be progressing slowly, it's hard to realize how fast you're really learning. As every day goes by, you're getting better – if you practice. There'll be times when you're shown something new, another chord or rhythm, and you'll feel you've gone right back to square one. Don't lose heart. Just remember what you can already do. Remember how it was the first time you picked up the instrument! Keep at it. There's a lot of enjoyment ahead.

Finally, before you leave your first lesson, make sure your know how to get the instrument in tune. This applies mainly to string instruments. There are six strings to get right on a guitar!

There's a fairly simple way you'll be shown to do it, but you do need that musical ear – being able to tell the difference between two notes, remember? There are various gadgets you can get to help with this; but eventually you should be able to hear when it's right.

Forming a Band

Hopefully by now you've met up with several people who've been learning to play an instrument at the same time as you. If you can now play reasonably well, you might have thought of teaming up to form a band.

Think about the instruments you're all playing. Will they sound good together? Also, do you think you could get on well with these other people?

Choosing the right individuals to form the line-up of a band is extremely important; not only because they are – or could be – good musicians. Think seriously about what

they're like as people. Do they get easily irritated, annoyed or bored? Ideally the members of the band should all get on with each other. At the very least, no one should be a constant irritation.

If one person is quick to give orders all the time, other members may get fed up with being told what to do. If one person is good as far as ideas go, and you all agree with them, then you might all decide that person should be the leader. But you must then accept whatever decisions he or she makes. If you can't all agree on something, then you could take a vote. This will be a problem if there's an even number of you though, say six. You could end up with a tie – three to three. How will you sort that out?

There are quite a few all-female groups around nowadays. And of course there are hundreds, maybe thousands, of mixed groups. It shouldn't be necessary to say that everyone in the group, male or female, should be taken seriously.Hopefully this will seem obvious to you. Sadly though, there's still quite a bit of sexism about, with some men putting down women. Don't lose out by having this stupid way of thinking creep into the way you deal with each other as musicians.

Another important thing about the band is that you should all share the same musical interests. You should all know what kind of music you want to play. It's also a good thing to make sure you're playing with others of similar skill, otherwise you'll just get frustrated and maybe even kicked out.

In the band, the songwriters have the power. However good a musician you are, you can be replaced. Therefore try your hand at writing some songs.

Beware of people who think too much of themselves. They just want a band behind them to show off. They might be a laugh at first, but later they can make your life a misery. This description doesn't fit you, does it?

Ego-trippers can break up a group or a Breaks Centre. It's important that everyone gets a break and that no one's chances of fun or learning are spoiled by some thoughtless ego-tripping twit.

Rehearsing/Rehearsal Rooms

Up until now everybody has been busy playing their own instruments, probably at home. Drummers face the most trouble here as far as noise goes. It is possible though, to play without waking up the entire road: get some practice pads – pieces of felt put over the drums to cut down the noise.

The electric guitarist and keyboard player will plug headphones into their amps so only they can hear the noise. However, the singer will practise a heavy rock yell no louder than a whisper; the acoustic guitarist will strum the rhythmn softly; and any saxophone, clarinet, recorder, flute or kazoo players will only be able to puff very gently.

If the members of the band feel confident of their musical ability, then now is the time to play together and make some noises.

This involves searching high and low for a rehearsal space. There are lots of ways of going about solving this problem. The easiest is to ask the bands you know of in clubs about where they go to rehearse. Chances are that they're paying for somewhere. They're probably earning money and can afford to do that. Perhaps you can't. So you should try to get a place for nothing if you can. It won't be easy, but it's worth a try.

This is where you take to the streets. Look for empty warehouses, basements or maybe a spare room under a shop. Ask around to find out who owns it and see if they're prepared to let you use it. If it's owned by the Council then you've got a better chance than with a private landlord. If you look hard enough you might well be lucky.

Supposing then that you've got a place. The first thing to do is to find out how soundproof it is. When you're inside can you still hear traffic outside? Or planes? Set up the guitar and amp and leave someone behind playing and go outside to see if you can hear anything. What you've got to try to do is to stop all sound from that room reaching the outside.

If you're close to other houses, you'll get complaints from neighbours and pretty soon you'll have lost your space. Remember that not everyone is up when you are. Some people work shifts, others might be elderly. And people with babies have enough problems sleeping anyway. Don't wake anybody!

If you can hear the sound from outside, then there's quite a lot to do to make it quieter.

If there are any holes in the building then the sound will gush out, just like water from a sieve. Find and block these holes. With all that done you should notice a lot of difference.

The next thing to think about is the way the room reacts to sound. The acoustics of one room will be different to those of another – like the way your voice sounds different if

you sing in your bedroom or your bathroom. In some rooms you have more unwanted echo than in others. So then, you need to get rid of this echo from your rehearsal room.

To do that you need to cover up as many hard surfaces as you can. Walls, doors, ceilings and the floor should be covered with some kind of soft surface.

Floors are fairly easy. Hunt around for old bits of carpet. You can also tack some carpet over the door entrance itself so all the cracks at the edges are covered. Make sure it's no problem to get out though!

So, how do you get anything up on the ceiling – and what? This is simpler than it seems. It does take a while though. You'll have to ask your family and neighbours to save their empty egg-boxes for you. A restaurant might be a good place to try as well. Then you have to put them up. But, as with any other alterations you might want to make, check with the owner. These egg boxes aren't for sound-proofing. They're to change the acoustics in the room by absorbing the high frequencies.

Another useful thing to look out for is some sort of wall-tiling. There's a kind called acoustic tiling. It's expensive though. Hunt around some more. You might find a shop which uses tiles to display goods, so you might get them cheap because they're shopworn; or shops which sell these might even give you their chipped ones! Ask.

Some of the sound-proofing materials you bring into the room may catch fire easily. You need to take extra precautions to check this out. Get some fire extinguishers – you'll need one for electrical fires and one for normal types of fire. You can get some useful advice here from your local fire station.

If you must smoke, then make sure you have some ashtrays. However, with all that equipment around it's probably best to wait until you step outside for a break before lighting up. Make certain the wiring of your plugs is safe and that the power points in the room are safe. Have an electrician check this out for you.

You now have some idea of the kind of place you need for a rehearsal space. You will have to keep searching till you find one. Find out what the other bands are doing. They may have discovered an amazing place you missed or they might still be looking. A good idea in this case is to think of

sharing the space. You won't all want to use it at the same time. Be fair. The thing to do is to write a short document that says you all agree to abide by a few simple rules. This will set out just how you go about sharing the space and maybe even the equipment and repairs.

It should answer the following points:

- **how much is paid by each person or band**
- **who has first choice of rehearsal time**
- **who has which days and hours**
- **who is allowed to use what equipment**
- **who will pay how much if equipment breaks down**
- **who gets it fixed**

Sort something like that out at the start and have it signed by everybody. It will save a lot of aggro later on.

When working or sharing space with other bands, there are three 'golden rules' to remember:

1. Don't take another band's gear.
2. Keep quiet when they're tuning up.
3. Always be on time.

There's more advice on setting up a rehearsal room and on sharing it successfully in the Breaks Centre section of this book, starting on page 73

The rehearsal space must be made secure. Make sure there are good locks on the door – like heavy duty lever locks – and perhaps add a strong padlock. Your local hardware shop or the crime prevention officer at the local police station can advise you on the best means of securing any door. If you want to get insurance cover for anything you're likely to leave in the room, the company might also insist that – the windows are barred, there's a lock-up cupboard and maybe even a burglar alarm.

This often gets overlooked until it's too late. Insurance may sound boring, but it's better than losing everything and never getting the money back!

If you're using someone else's building, chances are you'll be covered by their insurance. Check this out first thing. The things you need to insure against are – any damage to the building or property in it; or if anyone gets hurt (this is called Public Liability Insurance).

If you have any valuable equipment you should insure this against loss, theft or damage as well. Remember that if you use a car or van to get around, you must let your insurance company know what you're doing, otherwise the equipment won't be covered unless it's locked up in the building.

Also, of course, you have to insure your van at least against hitting other people or things. (This is called Third Party Liability.) Your best bet is to get in touch with a few insurance brokers (look them up in the Yellow Pages or your local directory). They advise you free of charge on what you need. Also shop around for the best deal with the insurance companies. Talk to more than one broker to check which one can get you the best deal from the companies.

Transport

You'll have to find your own transport. This is especially important when it comes to getting the gear to the rehearsal room. Unless you live right next door, you won't be able to use a wheelbarrow! If you also intend to play live in clubs someday, you'll need a van, though not full-time of course.

If none of you can drive, try and cadge lifts off your family or friends. If you share a space with other bands there's a greater chance of finding someone.

When you're ready with the cash and the absolute need, and if one of you can drive, then look around for a reasonably priced second-hand van. The rules for this are the same as for buying anything else second-hand. The person selling it is not a friendly adviser. Get someone with a good knowledge of vehicles to help you out.

Make sure the van isn't too big. Otherwise you'll probably be wasting petrol. Remember, though, if you eventually want to play in clubs, you'll need to be able to fit even more equipment into it than you now have.

Managers

When you started the group, perhaps you had a lot of friends around. Not all of them wanted to play an instrument or sing. Now is the time to ask them to help you with posters, leaflets, sound mixing and other jobs.

One important job that needs to be done is that of manager. You need someone you can all get on with easily, who's committed to you and who's honest.

Managers need to be good at arranging things. They should have a good line of chat. This will make it easier for them to be able to persuade people to listen to the band.

Managers should present themselves well and aim to make a good impression. It reflects on the band. If the manager looks a mess, people will think the band is a mess.

Later on, the manager's duties will include talking to journalists to get the band into the newspapers, sending out demo tapes, dealing with promoters, sorting out gigs for you and trying to get a record deal. Everyone in the band should understand about the money side. Take advice from outside people especially if your manager is inexperienced. A manager will have to look after the business side of running a band.

If everything works out fine with the manager, then for the sake of protection, it should be insisted that the band draw up a contract. This makes the manager, in effect, another member of the band. It makes it harder for, say, a record company to split the manager from the band and give you someone else to do the job.

Mixers

When the band plays live in a club it's necessary to balance the sound. This allows each instrument to be heard clearly and at the right level when the band plays together. For example, the drums shouldn't drown the sound of the bass, and the guitar shouldn't wipe out the singer's voice.

You use a mixer for this. On it are a number of sliding volume controls called faders. The person doing the mixing, also called the mixer, adjusts the controls until the correct balance is achieved. You won't be buying a mixer yet until you start playing in clubs. There's a lot to learn before you do. It's a good idea for you, or one or two friends, to think of learning how to be sound mixers. They need to know what kind of sound the band is trying to achieve. When you go to see bands playing in clubs, watch the sound mixers there.

Ask them questions. They'll explain what a mixer has to do to make the group sound like they do. Ask them to show you the differences that can be made to the sounds by just twiddling a few knobs. It's useful to know as much as you can about mixers before your band gets its own.

Demo Recordings

It will be very useful for you to make recordings of your rehearsal. This can be done simply by using a cassette machine stuck in the middle of the room. If it has one of those plug-in mikes, hang that from the ceiling. Don't have it too near any of the amps or drums. You need to hear each instrument. Be sure to set the level correctly so it doesn't over-record and distort the sound.

After the session, listen to the play-back. If you can, try to plug the cassette into a larger loudspeaker. This will make it easier for you to hear the deep bass and high cymbals. These are important rhythm points and the music may sound messy unless you can hear them.

Now you'll be able to find out how well the music fits together and whether or not you're all keeping perfect time. You'll then be able to try to improve. Perhaps you'll do that by changing slightly what each instrument is playing until it sounds better. For example, if the guitarist is attempting some wild 'freak out' solo, does it sound right? If not, perhaps something a little simpler should be tried.

These kinds of things will only be found out once you listen to tapes of yourselves. Some things you won't notice while you're playing, because you're too busy watching what your fingers are doing, or thinking about how the words go.

Everybody in the band should sit and listen to the tapes. You should all be honest and say what you think. Try to be constructive when you criticize. Make suggestions and don't make fun about other people's playing. If you get criticized, then don't get up-tight. Listen to see if it makes sense.

These tapes shouldn't be played to anyone else. They're for your use only. If other people heard them, you'd be explaining all the time how different it sounds in real life – how much better! So there's no point in playing someone a duff tape. If you want tapes to play to people, they ought to be of the best quality you can manage.

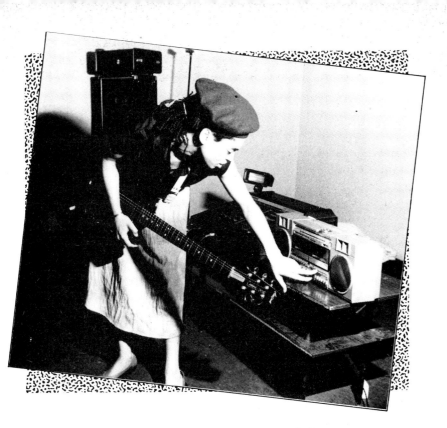

It's extremely useful to have a batch of demo tapes you can play to others without having to apologize for their quality. You might want friends or relations to hear what you sound like. You'll want them to hear you at your best.

If the tape quality is bad, people will think it's the way you play! Later on, these good tapes can be sent out to music papers to get reviewed, to record companies to try for a deal and to promoters to get you gigs.

Unfortunately the only way to get high-quality recordings is by getting hold of a high-quality and expensive tape-recorder and mixer. Your ghetto-blaster just won't do anymore.

Ideally you need a four-track reel-to-reel recorder and a small mixer with perhaps six or eight microphone inputs. Nearly as good are the new 'Portastudios' which are four-track cassette machines with small built-in mixers.

The particular type of four-track you need is the kind that lets you record onto each track separately. It must also allow you to listen to one track while recording on another. The most common four-track decks which do these things are made by TEAC and Fostex.

The advantage of four-track recording on a reel-to-reel or a portastudio is that you can first record instruments one at a time on separate tracks. Then you can add one track to another to build up your final sound. The mixer will also allow you to control the tone and level of each recording.

The process is basically the same as that used by the big studios, only they have fancier sixteen-track or even twentyfour-track recorders. Don't be fooled though; more expensive gear doesn't necessarily mean better music.

Four-track recorders, mixers and portastudios are very expensive to buy (see page 51). They can be hired commercially for short periods.

There are also many music workshops and arts centres that have this gear, and some hire it out cheaply. Multi-track recording is a lot of fun but needs some careful thought. So make sure you have someone who knows how to do it before you set up your first session. Otherwise you'll be wasting expensive recording time.

It's important that everyone in the band understands how to do mixing and recording; but making one of your friends a mixer for your recordings and gigs is a good idea.

In order to get a good recording you'll have to choose the right mikes and have them in the right places. You could find this out by experimenting, but it's better to get some help. Recordings made with well-placed mikes sound much better. They're also better than just plugging the instruments straight into the recorder. They sound much livelier and more like you sound when you play. By putting mikes in front of the amps you normally use, you can also use the effects you might have – things like fuzz pedals and echo for guitars.

Before you start recording it's a good idea to plan what you're going to do. Write it all down on a sheet of paper as a guide. When you've got the perfect demo, make some copies. You can send these to anyone you think needs to hear them. If they're going out to strangers, make sure you write the details on the tape box: the band's name, the manager's name, and an address and phone number so they can get in touch with you if they want to.

Finally some advice on the contents of the demo tape. You should have three songs which are all your own compositions. Don't just sing someone else's greatest hit. People should be able to judge your song-writing skills, not just how well you play.

Copyright

For each song you write, you hold the copyright. This stops anyone else from recording or performing it without your permission or without paying you for its use. If you send out a demo tape with original materials on it, you should mark it with a © symbol and write the composer's name plus the date and the year.

In practice it's extremely difficult to enforce copyright on music. The only thing that can be done to prove this is by sending a copy of the manuscript or tape to yourself by registered post. Keep it sealed and in a safe place. The postmark will prove it existed on a certain date. Then if you suddenly hear it on the radio, you're in a stronger position to take legal action.

The Mechanical Copyright Protection Society (MCPS) issues a leaflet advising on the subject of securing your copyright. Their address is listed at the end of this book. If you write a lot of songs and make money from them by having them performed in the theatre, on the radio or on television, then you can register as a composer with the MCPS. They'll collect the royalty payments for you.

Making Your Own Record

Whether as an individual band or as a collective, the time will come when you may want to make a record. There are good reasons for doing this.

A properly made record will look more impressive than a demo tape and it'll be easier to get people to listen to it – particularly media people. If you send one in to a radio station they might play it, even though they might not play demo tapes.

There are many companies around that can make your tape into a finished record. You have to make sure your tape is as near perfect as you can get it in every way – musically and technically. If you have a good tape, there are companies who will press these into a record for you. It's an interesting process. The tape needs to be mastered so that the volume is evenly controlled without something suddenly becoming too loud. This is to stop someone accidentally blowing up their hi-fi! From this master tape a lacquer is made and it is this that is used to press the records.

A typical cost for all this would be about £500 for a thousand singles. Prices do vary a lot, so check through the adverts in your papers. Some will even give you cheap time in a studio to make a really good recording as part of the deal.

That cost will include plain sleeves. If you want a design or photo on the sleeve you'll probably have to find a company that specializes in printing record sleeves. If you can produce your own design by some method of printing you'll save a lot of money and still have good results. A community centre might have a silkscreen printing machine or a darkroom so you can process any photos you want to use. Some Letraset will look better than anybody's handwriting, so you can spell out your band's name loud and clear.

Think of ways of making your band's sleeve stand out from the thousands of others in the record shops.

The pressing plant will put plain white labels in the middle of the records. If you want something different, then you'll have to design one and give it to the company to print up and put on. This will cost you more money but it might be easier than writing on the singles.

If you want to get this record into the shops, you have to approach one of the independent distributors. A list of these is included at the end of the book.

Advertising and Promotion

You may or may not think that promotion is very important. If your music is a hobby, you'll enjoy using it to entertain at youth groups, community activities and events. In this case all that matters is that people who want to see you know when and where you're playing.

If, on the other hand, you're hoping to get a backer or a record company to turn the group into a paying proposition, then promotion is something you've got to work on.

Promotion is important because it gets people to come to see you in the first place. That then gets you invited to other venues. Once you've got an audience, your promotion keeps them in touch with what you're doing. It builds a buzz around the group, a feeling that you're doing something or going somewhere. And if you're smart, you won't even have to pay for it.

Telling the Media Whenever you play, make sure you tell all the magazines which run free listings columns. Don't just tell the specialist music magazines. Contact the local newspaper as well. They'll be interested because your gig is local news. They need local news to sell their local advertising.

Send the details to them and ask if they want to run an article on you. If you say you've got black and white photos, they might be even more interested. They'll get a picture without having to pay a photographer, unless some ruling prevents them. Since the paper won't run an article on you every week, make sure you pick a week when you've got a gig coming up. Then the article will help promote the gig and copies of it will be useful later on.

So remember to cut out the article with the date and name of the paper attached and photocopy it. Then you can always send a copy to people – perhaps with the demo tapes. There's nothing worse than getting into print and finding out next week that no one's hung on to a copy of the article.

It's nice to see your names in print but don't let it go to your heads. By tomorrow several thousand other people will have seen their names in print as well. It's all forgotten except by you and your friends the next day. The thing you have to do is make good use of copies of the article to promote yourselves in future.

Another organization you should keep in touch with is

your local radio station. Keep them informed about your gigs. Whatever type of music you play, listen to their programmes and get to know which one plays your kind. If you hear that they play demo tapes, then you should send them one of yours.

If you do, the tape is best recorded in stereo. It should be on reel-to-reel which runs at fifteen inches per second. If you're certain that the station doesn't play demos, then it's probably still worth doing. You never know until you try. Maybe they haven't heard a tape as good as yours! Since reel-to-reel is expensive you might try to get it returned to you by adding a note and sending them a stamped addressed envelope.

If you find someone who does play your type of music, you might like to try phoning them to see if you can arrange to meet. This will give you a real chance to play your tape and explain yourself. You might be able to get DJs or music journalists down to your gigs if you send them some complementary or VIP tickets to get them in free. Don't overdo it though – you need the money!

Posters and Word of Mouth If you've got posters, use them a few days before gigs. If they go up too far in advance, people will get too used to the image before the date; they'll stop looking at them. Put up as many as you can where people pass by who might come to your gig. There's no point in advertising your gig in front of a pensioners' club.

Put them up in the area around where you'll be playing. Pubs, discos, local schools, youth centres and maybe even the local record shop are good places for your posters. Check your local council for the rules on fly-posting. In some places it's illegal. Use your discretion.

Posters only remind people of a gig – posters don't make them go. It's important for people to hear of the gig by word of mouth too. It's always a good idea to phone as many people as you can on the day of the gig. This does as much as anything to guarantee a hard core of friends and fans.

Remember, posters are only reminders. They don't sell things very well. Word of mouth is what gets things going and gets people coming to hear you. It's worth asking the venue if they're prepared to do any advertising. Sometimes they are. If, for example, they take a regular weekly spot in a magazine or newspaper, they might include the band's name in it for the night you're playing.

Tell the gig organizer how much promotion you're doing yourselves. If you get local newspaper or radio spots, they should be delighted. But don't expect them to say 'thanks' or to pay you for it. On the other hand you could try to get a written agreement that they'll pay for leaflets, posters and adverts.

If you do even half the things listed above, you should pull a bigger crowd than a better-known band playing down the street. A good-sized and friendly crowd often means you play a better gig than normal. This might mean that next time you'll be able to do a better gig at another place. People with talent grow with experience.

Remember, bigger isn't always better. It depends on the kind of music you play, the acoustics of the place and whether you're ready to play well in front of a live audience. It may look easy, but it can be nerve-racking. At the very least, you have to be well rehearsed.

Visuals

Of the hundreds, maybe thousands, of bands that gig around the country every week, some make much more of an impression than others. Obviously the ones with record deals are more familiar. But even among the unsigned bands there are some whose names you see around more often than others. You might associate them with a particular poster or photo. There are those whose names you remember even if you've never heard any of their music.

A lot of the ideas that people get about bands have as much to do with the way they look as the way they sound. This goes for established chart acts as well as brand new bands. If a demo tape has a good picture or design on it, people may react better to the music because they think you've taken some care and pride in what you do. If a band has a good appearance on stage, it makes for a better gig, because it looks good as well as sounding good.

Imagine a record company's employees who have to listen to hundreds of cassettes by new bands every day. If a cassette comes with a photo of the band, the people who listen to it are likely to get a much clearer impression of that particular band than of all the others. They also have something else to refer to when they talk to others about it.

If you have a strong visual style, you can attract both record companies and record buyers much more easily than groups without a clear image. One good design or photo, if it's put on enough posters or stickers, can make a name stick in the minds of thousands of people.

Some musicians feel that visual image is 'just hype', and has 'nothing to do with the music'. Certainly the image should fit the band and not simply be a gimmick. With an image and sound that people like and remember, then a snowball effect starts to happen. If a band develops a following based on its musical and visual style, it will get more opportunities to play, to survive and to develop musically.

The image needn't cost very much at all if the ideas are really good. Your clothes, posters and photos can be as eye-catching as those of bands which have spent thousands of pounds on promotion. You might drop in on your local repertory theatre or alternative theatre. They have designers and directors who put shows on stage all the time. They'll probably help you for nothing if you simply ask. On the other hand, if you really think that performing is only about the music, and you hate the idea of visual publicity, then stay as you are.

But remember, if you ignore it, you are definitely missing part of what performing is about. It's one of the best and cheapest ways for a new band to get attention; and it's one that's in your control.

Some of the things you could think about using are outlined below:

Photos It's very useful to have a stack of band photos available. You can give them to anyone who wants to use them. You can even send them as postcards. You may not see the results straight away. They lie around in houses and offices and get seen casually by people you wouldn't have reached otherwise.

All you really need is one photo negative that you're happy with. You can run off as many copies of it as you can afford. To get that photo, you need to find a good photographer. This isn't as difficult as it might sound.

Start with asking the editor of your local newspaper for names. Find out who left a local photography course last year. Most young photographers really want to get involved with bands, especially bands that are going to use the photos for promotion. This is publicity for the photographer as well.

If you can't find a freelance photographer by asking around, try to get a student from the local technical college, art school, arts centre or adult education centre. These

places also have photographic darkrooms, which means you could learn to do your own printing. That's obviously going to make it much cheaper.

Whoever the photographer is, explain to him or her what sort of picture you have in mind. Make sure they come to see you rehearse and play in order to get a feel for your style.

Also make sure you write up an agreement with the photographer. You should be absolutely clear about whether you own the negative or not. At the very least, make sure you have the right to print and use unlimited copies without further payment.

The cheapest way to do a photo session is to use black and white film. You then get a 'contact sheet' of strips of small prints made up from the negatives. This allows you to choose the best picture without having to pay for printing them all up full size. After you choose the picture you want from the contact sheet, you'll probably be able to print up stacks of copies just for the cost of materials. This depends, of course, on your deal with the photographer.

Leaflets If there's a photocopier that you can get the use of cheaply, or even free, it would be a great help in producing leaflets. It's especially useful for flysheets and handouts before gigs. There can be black and white sheets with a simple design, the name of the band, and when and where you're playing. You can also use photocopied sheets as small posters, although they have to be larger than a standard A4 sheet to be really eye-catching. If you're not doing too many, you can add some patches of colour by hand with felt-tip pens.

Some schools and colleges now have colour copying machines. Copies on these are quite expensive, but they can produce great results. Try to get the use of one of these at cost. You can make prints of colour slides. You could also colour in a black and white poster and then copy it on one of these.

Leaflets run off on a photocopier or duplicator are probably the most cost-effective means of advertising your band.

Silkscreen Silkscreening posters is more expensive than photocopying, but the sheet of paper you use can be bigger. And a silkscreen poster can also have as many colours as you're willing to do. If you work out your own designs, and can find a printer at your local technical college, youth or arts centre, or community printshop, then you'll be able to do plenty of these.

Using one colour is the cheapest of course, but it can be any colour. Make sure that the information in the design is clear and striking – when, where and the names. There's no point in getting everyone to notice a poster if nobody knows what it's for.

If you have the money and you want to do a long run of hundreds or thousands of leaflets or posters, then you'll want to have them printed on an off-set litho machine. Don't just go to one printer – shop around. Ring three different printers and tell them exactly what you want – size, numbers, colours and type of paper and have them give you a price for the job.

Videos A video-tape of a group is a very impressive thing to have. It's nowhere near as expensive as you might think. If you can get hold of a home video-camera and recorder

(VHS or Betamax), you can simply fix it in front of the stage and let it carry on recording through a gig or rehearsal. Otherwise you can get someone to work the camera and record the group while you're playing.

All you need to check is that there's enough light (the camera tells you this), and that the sound doesn't distort when you do your sound check. Everything else is automatic. Remember, never point a video-camera straight at a light, or it will burn onto the picture and tube.

The sound and picture quality you get from a basic video-recorder isn't amazing, but you can do it for the cost of the tape (about a fiver). One important thing is that it impresses gig organizers and journalists. Another is that you will see how you look to others.

Remember, just like finding a young photographer at college or one trying to work freelance, you might find a video-maker or graphic designer in the same situation. By giving them a chance to do their thing and get experience, you're helping them as well as your own group. Everyone needs that first break to get started. Otherwise you're trapped in Catch 22 – you can't get a gig or a job unless you've had a gig or a job!

PA Gear

The amplifiers and speakers you have now are probably not loud enough to let everyone in a big hall hear you. If you want to play in larger venues or to larger audiences you need to use a PA (Public Address) system.

Some venues have their own PA system; but more often bands have to hire or bring their own along. If you're playing with other bands on the same night you may be able to use their PA. Perhaps you can hire one together. In either case you must make some agreement with them well before the gig.

The rough cost of a PA for a few instruments, three mikes and an electric guitar would be about £25–£30 for the night. The hire company will provide an engineer to set it up. The engineer is useful because setting up a PA is quite complicated. Also there are a lot of bits and pieces of equipment that may be new to you. For a five- or six-piece rock or reggae band much more gear will be needed. It will cost somewhere between £40 and £80 a night to hire.

The big speakers you need are split into three kinds. They're called bass-bins or cabs, mid-bins and horns. You'll need a pair of each to cope with the bass notes, the mid-range notes and the high frequencies. You'll also need a crossover unit to split up the sound into these frequency ranges. A mixer is now needed to control the various sound levels.

The speaker stacks will be out in front of the stage. In order for the band to hear what they're doing, you'll each need a small monitor speaker. That goes for singers too. These monitors are placed around the front of the stage so that each musician can hear what he or she is playing.

All the microphones must be plugged into a stage box. A cable from this then connects them all to the mixer. The drum kit will now need several mikes – ideally one for each drum and one or two for the cymbals. Yards of thick expensive cable called multicore are needed to connect everything together.

Power amps are needed to drive the speakers. These will need to be either 400 or 800 watts. The amount of power you will need will vary according to the size of hall you're playing in. The PA hire company or promoter will be able to help you sort this out.

If you're wanting to buy a PA rig you've got to be prepared to shell out about £2500 if it's for a reasonably sized group. You'll need all the advice you can get. If you start to buy one bit by bit, make sure it will all match up at the end. Hopefully, though, by the time you start buying a PA, you'll have used them often enough in clubs to be very familiar with them.

Check with the other new bands in your area. It might be quicker for you to club together for one when the time comes. You don't need a PA to start.

Gigs

After much rehearsing, the time will come when you feel you're ready to play in front of a crowd of people. Perhaps invite some friends along to one of your rehearsals to try to get used to the idea of having other people watch you. This is a good way to start.

But remember, your friends are on your side. They may know some of the songs already if you've played them a demo tape. They might react more strongly to those than some they don't know. This doesn't mean those are your best songs. Your first real audience won't have heard any of your songs. You have to think of ways of keeping their attraction. Playing well and being interesting to look at aren't the only answers.

You should also decide on a running order for the songs to be performed. The sound balance may not be right when you begin the gig, so it's not worth wasting your best song as an opener. But you'll need something exciting so that everyone will know you've begun. People might be in some far corner of the room chatting to friends. If you're too low-key at the start they might just think it's still the taped music in the background.

So when planning a gig there are several things to consider. It's a good idea not to run too many slow songs together; try to vary your material during your sets. Any audience will need a break from the loud stuff now and again, but think carefully where you slot in the slower songs. Try to arrange the order of songs so that the gig gradually works up to a climax. This should, hopefully, leave the audience wanting more.

If you do get asked to do an encore then don't be ashamed of repeating any numbers. Pick the strongest ones. At the end, you'll probably be feeling a lot more confident. You should be able to perform them even better than the first time. The audience will remember them and hopefully will respond well.

No matter how well things go in front of your friends, you

need practice in front of strangers. You can learn something from the way they react – or don't react, as the case may be. You might be able to get to play at a youth centre during some event.

Perhaps there's a benefit concert coming up in your area for the 'Punk Parking Ticket Offenders'. Benefits of all kinds are quite common in parks during the summer. The organizers won't worry about your lack of experience; nobody's paying to see you. You just add another name to the bill. This will make it look as if they've done a super job in getting so many bands to play free. Be careful where you leave the van or you'll need a benefit too!

The first gig in an established venue will probably be one that you or your manager fixes up. Perhaps the promoter heard a demo tape. Never play promoters a tape that you've spent hours recording and re-recording until it sounds as good as a record. This advice may sound strange, but when you play live, you won't be able to reproduce this sound so you'll only disappoint them. They might think you were trying to fool them and might not ask you back.

The same thing holds true if you're playing your first ever gig. It's better to admit it's the first. They'll understand. Most promoters are prepared to give new bands a chance. You'll only begin as a support act and you probably won't get any billing.

If the promoter is going to give you a chance, then don't waste it. Have a chat well before the gig and check on all the details. Find out for certain that you'll be able to use the PA – either the main band's or one the promoter has hired for use by both bands – the 'house' PA.

Check what time you should arrive for the load-in and sound-check. Time for this is nearly always short. The promoter has a lot of things to sort out on the day of the gig. Find out anything you want to know beforehand so that you won't make a nuisance of yourself.

Discuss with the main band what you're using in the way of equipment. For example, if you both need the same on-stage amps (the back line), it could be left up for use by both bands. This will save time between bands when you otherwise have to hump all one band's gear off and the other band's on. Usually the main band's gear will be used because their stuff is likely to be better than yours. Hopefully they won't be snobbish about your using it.

It's worth thinking of safeguarding your gear at the gig. In the darkness and confusion on-stage, it's easy to leave a piece of gear behind thinking it belongs to the other band. It's also possible to pick up someone else's gear accidentally or to have a piece of yours go in the same way.

There are a couple of useful things you can do to prevent this. Wind some coloured sticky tape around your cables and leads. Amps and instrument cases should be marked with the band's name or the player's name. The band's name is best, because whatever other band you play with will know that it should be left alone.

The best way of marking equipment is to make a spray stencil. This can be made from thin cardboard by simply cutting out the letters of your band's name. You then hold this against the surface you want marked, and paint through the gaps with some waterproof paint. You could

also use a paint spray for this. A small tin of car paint spray would be useful.

The next thing to consider will be the mixing. The main band will almost certainly have their own person to do their mixing. If your mixers have managed by then to gain some live experience, then they could do your sound for you. If not, trust the other band's mixer. Sound mixers take their job seriously. Their only aim is to coax the best sound possible from the mixing desk.

Support bands normally only have a very short sound-check. The mixer will need to hear you playing together so that a good, balanced sound can be worked out. Time will be very limited so there must be no messing around. Two or three songs should be performed – maybe a fast one and a slow one. This will give the mixer an idea of how you'll play during the gig.

If there's no time for you to have a sound-check, don't moan about it. The main band's sound-check will be done first. They might have problems with their equipment causing a delay; they might not be in the right mood for you to ask them to hurry up.

Their mixer will be experienced enough to have you sounding good by the end of your first number. Discuss what you're doing. Give the mixer a list of the song titles to keep track of things. State clearly when you're using different instruments or back-up vocals.

An important thing to sort out at the sound-check is that you can all hear your own monitors clearly. This allows you to carry on even if the sound out front isn't right yet.

When you reach the agreed time to go on stage, go straight on. Never be late. If you are, you'll be holding up the main band. If the venue has to close at a certain time, they'll have to shorten their set. The promoter will be unlikely to ask you back. If there's no one in the club, you still have to go on. You may have to get used to playing for a while to four bare walls.

As a support band, you can't expect to make much money. Your wages will almost always come from money taken on the door. This has to be divided between the main band and your band. Before you even start, you may already owe the promoter about £15 towards the cost of the hired PA. Be prepared to cover this cost if you don't take much money at the door.

Always make sure you're absolutely clear just how much you'll be paid before you do the gig. It's the promoter's responsibility to pay you. Appoint one of the band or your manager to collect the money at the end of the gig. That will stop the promoter from giving you the runaround by telling you the money was given to someone else.

If you were promised a flat rate, say £50, then be sure you get this amount. If the promoter argues that only a few people came, it makes no difference. You're still owed £50, if it was a flat-rate, no-deductions agreement. Whatever your payment is for the gig, make sure you get it in cash before you leave the venue.

Here are the things to consider before doing a gig:

Money
- **How much will we be paid?**
- **Does that depend on the size of the audience?**
- **When do we get paid?**

Expenses
- **Who pays for the PA?**
- **Who pays for the lighting?**
- **Are there any other expenses or deductions?**

Sound
- **Who mixes?**
- **When can we meet beforehand?**
- **Will we get a sound-check?**
- **How long will it be?**

If you play a good gig and the promoter is happy, you'll probably be asked back. You can then discuss publicity. Say that you want to put up posters to advertise the next gig. Often promoters are willing to split the cost of a couple of hundred posters, which is well worthwhile.

There are a couple of books which might be very useful to anyone trying to organize gigs. They contain nationwide lists of promoters, venues, equipment hire companies, record companies and broadcasting organizations. These and other useful books are listed at the back of this book, on page 127

The Musicians' Union Once the band is gigging it might be worthwhile joining the Musicians' Union (MU). Most professional musicians are members. For young musicians making very little money, membership of the MU costs about £20 a year.

If you get into a mess, like with a promoter who doesn't want to pay the amount promised, you could drop a hint that you're going to mention it to the MU. Then the promoter will probably pay you what was promised. Otherwise you should take it to the Union.

The MU has set up a minimum rate for work. This means that musicians doing session work or playing in a touring band mustn't be paid less than that rate. Sadly though, there are no minimum rates for bands on the club circuit. But still, it might be useful to have some protection anyway.

If you should get into any serious trouble, the MU may also be able to help you with its own solicitor. That could save you a lot of money.

Record Deals

Some bands just enjoy playing as a hobby. These are better off ignoring the business side of music altogether. Trying to be a commercial outfit can mean losing a lot of the original enjoyment. Others will find that they might be able to make their band pay for itself. They might even be able to buy new and better equipment. A large part of this success will be based on making an effort with advertising and promotion; and on keeping their 'hit-list' informed about the band and its gigs.

Some groups or individuals will actually want to try to make a career out of music. This means turning the band (or yourself) into a business. This, in turn, means getting a recording contract. For every group that makes it this far, there are literally thousands that don't.

It's true, of course, that a band with a record company deal can make a lot of money. But often this money takes a long time to come in – usually two years – if ever. A new band might make more on the dole for those two years. And that applies even if their first few singles are hits! All that expensive studio time can look inviting; but when you have to spend ten hours a day there, it's more like a job than a hobby.

Also, if you don't like the idea of sitting around with lawyers and business types for hours discussing contracts, then signing a deal might not be as exciting as you imagine. All in all, turning professional is hard work, and for that reason not all bands want to do it. It's something you ought to think long and hard about, but only when a real chance is sitting in front of you. Then get some good advice from someone outside of the deal. Don't dream. Do everything you can to make your own break.

If you think you would be happy spending all your time and energy on your music for at least a few years to see if you can break through, then you ought to find out what a record contract is. It's actually a number of different deals. These can be made separately or together. Here are the basic ones.

Recording This part of the deal is a promise of studio time to make a master recording which can be released as a single. The record company will tell you that they're going to give you an advance. A typical figure would be about £20,000. This is not pocket money or for your salaries. All the costs for hiring or buying equipment, touring, hotel bills, studio time and promotion will have to come from this money. The company is, in effect, lending you £20,000.

The record companies make sure that you get say 4p for each single you sell. So it will take you a long time to repay them their £20,000. The record companies make sure that you stay with them for a long time to give themselves the smallest possible chance of losing money.

A usual deal is for you to sign for five years with an option at the end of that time. That means that after five years, if they're not happy with you they can write you out of the deal. It's their option! If you wanted to leave, you probably wouldn't be able to. You'd have to go to a solicitor to get you out and it would cost a lot of money.

Get an independent solicitor to check any deal before you sign it. It's difficult to get out of a bad deal. Don't rush to sign. If the record company's asked you to sign, then they must really want you. They'll just have to wait.

Make sure what kind of wage they're going to pay you. This is a kind of 'pocket money' you receive in addition to the advance on the income from royalties. You might be surprised, but even some of the bands in the charts at the moment are living on this money alone. It's usually only about £40 per week!

Management Most groups, once they turn professional, sign a management contract. This is when you formally state in writing that you'll pay your manager something like 20 per cent of your earnings. The manager will handle most of the day-to-day finances and paperwork, and makes all sorts of decisions. You should make sure you understand everything and check on it regularly. Sometimes the manager is involved with the creative side too, which could mean a higher percentage fee.

While you probably want to carry on having the person who's been managing you from the start, the record company will have other ideas. Often they have a pool of managers who each look after two or three of the bands on that label. You might worry about whether or not they've got enough time to spend on you. If you have any doubts, then tell the company.

The same goes if you want to keep your old manager. Tell them you'll only sign the recording contract if you're allowed to keep your manager on. Make sure your manager can really handle things in this new league before insisting on this though.

Promotion If you sign with a record company, remember they also control the record after it's made. They're responsible for promoting it – giving it a decent sleeve, doing posters and trying to interest the music press in writing something about you. They also produce some displays for the shops to use. The record company will have a video made for use on TV.

If the record isn't properly promoted, then very few people will even know it has been released. Sadly, this is the fate of too many records. The record company's promotions department is also responsible for 'plugging' the record – persuading DJs and producers to play it on the radio. Nowadays the record companies don't always do this themselves. They might get a full-time plugger to work for you.

Often these freelance pluggers can get the best results. Sometimes they may not even be paid unless the single reaches a certain position in the charts; so they have to work extra hard! There can be problems with them though. If a plugger is working on several records at once, perhaps some by famous bands, they may not have much time left to promote your record. They also might be on tour with a band or even out of the country!

Ask the record company what else the plugger is going to be doing. If you're not happy with the answer, then say so. Let the company know how much you're aware of what's going on. Don't let them think they can fool you.

Publishing This is a very important deal. It's best not to make it with the record company, although it might mean more money if you do.

The publishing deal concerns the songs themselves. Part of the money made from each record goes to the songwriter. Therefore you'll make more money writing your own songs.

If you sing someone else's song, you have to pay them a big slice of what you earn for recording it. If anyone else sings one of your songs, they have to pay you. A good publishing deal will make sure that you get all the money you're entitled to. If the publishing deal is with a company other than the one you're signed to, it stops either one having too much control.

It is also important who you credit as the songwriter. Sometimes this will be just one or two band members. Maybe one wrote the music and the other did the lyrics. If their names are written on the label, they will be the only ones to get the extra money.

It's quite common though for the group's name to be credited; and in those cases everyone will get an equal amount. In this situation, if the band should break up or if a member leaves, it will be necessary to change the contract. This might involve legal fees to change it so that the ex-members keep getting paid for the songs they've worked on. New members will be paid only for the new material they help create.

As with the record contract, make sure you get an independent 'music-biz' lawyer to study the deal carefully. The Musicians Union or the Law Society can help you find one. Don't go to a solicitor recommended by the company you're dealing with.

Independent Record Labels Besides the major record companies, there are hundreds of small, independent labels. They don't usually sign up bands for any length of time. Many of these companies might only release one or two records by a group. This means that you're free to get on with whatever else you're doing with anyone else you want to work with.

You can go to them with a demo tape of two songs that you think will make a good single. If they like it, they may put up the money for you to be able to record it in a studio.

When it's made, they'll then see that it gets out into the shops. If they think a lot of your band though, they might insist on signing you up before anybody else does.

Independent labels can't usually pay huge advances, so you'll probably only be tied for a short time to let you make a few records. They may not be able to pay you as much in wages as a major label can – if at all.

Remember to find out the details before you sign any contract. As with the major record companies, get an independent music-biz lawyer to go over the deal carefully before you take the pen from your pocket.

Many bands feel much better and safer with an independent label. Usually only one or two bands are signed at any one time. This means they can put in a lot of effort to get your band and its record off the ground.

In the past, the main problem with independents was their lack of success in distribution and promotion. These days though, things are getting better. Many of the independents have linked up with one or two big distribution companies to get their records into the shops. And pluggers are now more prepared to take on bands signed up with independents.

You may hear people say that bands on independent record labels don't have any success. That's not true. The majority of reggae releases are on independents. In the rock world there have been dozens of groups on independents who've had chart success – bands like King Kurt, The Cocteau Twins, New Order and The Smiths are just a few examples.

The names and addresses of the independent record companies in your region can be found by getting in contact with the Independent Labels Association (ILA) (see page 115). They have a list of all the independent companies on a computer. You can use this service to get in touch with the ones most likely to be interested in your type of music.

If you make a record with an independent label, the ILA will mail out copies of that single to radio stations and promote it. For a fee of £85 they'll promote two singles like this for a year.

Because independent labels can offer you a one-off deal, they are particularly useful if you want to make a compilation album with some of the bands in your area. You might want to do this when you've got a Breaks Centre going. Or this could be one way to get people to see how they can benefit from getting together to set up a Breaks Centre.

There are a lot of other reasons for setting up a centre for young bands in your area. Part Two of this book is about how to set up a Breaks For Young Bands Centre.

Indians in Moscow are a five-piece band from the outskirts of Hull. Last year they made their own record and were signed to a small independent company. That first release, 'Naughty Miranda', has sold 32,000 copies so far – helped by appearances on the TV programme 'The Tube'. The band have since released two more singles and have staged their own mini-tour of Britain to promote them.

"With equipment it depends so much on what you can afford but the best thing is to know your budget and get the best you can. When you're starting out you should

always get someone with experience to check out what you're buying. Especially if it's second-hand from somebody's house. Always with your first guitars you're ripped off 'cos you buy something new. We've bought one for £200 and then realized for the same money we could have got an older Gibson that's just as good and will always keep its value.

We haven't got our own P.A. On gigs we've played, the promoters have usually hired one or there's a permanent house PA. Generally you won't have to hire one unless you're putting on the gig yourself. We've got someone who comes round with us to do the sound mixing.

Be careful about promoters. We've just done this tour and found in some places that the promoter didn't do any advertising, so we ended up playing to half empty halls. So it's well worth talking to the promoter about splitting the cost of advertising. It's a shame but some promoters can be a bit dodgy, so it's good to have a manager or someone to hassle them for you.

A lot of bands have no interest in the finance side of things and consequently get no money. We've just done this rock-bottom sort of tour but our manager has been a huge help to us.

A good way to get contacts with record companies is through local radio 'cos they're dealing with those people all the time. The local papers are also very important 'cos you can build up your own little scrapbook of cuttings to show people. We found that by pressing our own record we had a much better chance of getting it heard. To save sending off to record companies you can ring them and make an appointment to see them. You'll see them eye to eye and have a chance to hear what they think.

Being in a working band is honestly hard work. We have to work every day of the week – doing gigs, rehearsing, recording, doing artwork, travelling up motorways in the van and, lately, more and more interviews.

It's still fun though and the glamour hasn't really worn off yet. We've even been asked for our autographs!"

Some words from Captain Sensible

It could be said that Captain Sensible represents the lunatic fringe of pop/rock owing to his wacky sense of humour. Fame came overnight for him with the release of his first solo album in 1982. From this came a number one chart single – a jolly version of 'Happy Talk'. Besides this success, the Captain is a member of The Damned; he's been involved with them since 1976. Ever since then, the band have been making records and touring to please their many fans. Mike Lambert did the following interview with Captain Sensible.

"Hello, Captain here. 'First I've got a bit to say about gear. A lot of people go out and buy gear 'cos it's got a name or it's big – especially heavy metal or punk groups. They like lots of gear, lots of amps, loads of noise and all that. The first drawback is you'll go deaf within a couple of years – and you don't want to do that if you're in the music business.

"Second, if you just get yourself a little combo that sounds

nice it'll be cheaper, easier to carry around and loud enough when you put it through the PA. You don't need a lot of noise on stage. I don't use big gear myself. I've only got a small combo with a speaker in it.

"Usually it's no trouble sharing another band's gear. We've done gigs where we've used the support band's backline of amps as a PA when ours didn't arrive. It's a shame, but too many people are full of the old routine like 'we're the stars' and getting all snobbish. We've always lent out the bass gear and drums; but not my amp 'cos it's very old and a bit temperamental. I would if I could though.

"A couple of tips for fellow guitar players. If you're inclined to sweat a bit on stage, I reckon you should change the strings every night. To hell with the expense. It's really embarrassing breaking strings on stage. If you just leave the guitar in its case overnight and you sweated all over it before, you'll break the strings next time you play it, especially if you play heavy-handed music like I do. For bass players: if your strings lose their 'twang', you can stick them for five minutes in boiling water, dry them off, put them on and they'll sound as good as new.

"About going on stage: I think it's really important for people to communicate with the audience. I hate seeing groups that just introduce the songs. They ought to tell the audience a bit about themselves – it's good for the vibes! The last thing they ought to do is say, 'It's great to be back,' or 'You're the greatest audience we've ever had,' or even worse, 'Do ya feel a-a-alrrri-i-i-ght.' Dump those clichés!

"Record companies? My first advice is to form your own label, or failing that, don't just go for smaller companies thinking that small is beautiful, even though I do say, 'thank God for Independents.' In my opinion the small labels are the same as the big ones. They've got the same sort of people and the same motives. Don't go for a small one 'cos it's groovy or a big one 'cos it's got more clout. Just go on the impression you get from the people. It's the old thing, no matter what the geezer says, don't let him rush you into it. Always get someone else to look at the contract. The MU can help you with a lawyer to check it for nothing.

"If you make it as far as a recording studio (and good luck!), I think people should always watch the producer and engineer and learn, 'cos it's all about finding your way round the business. The best tip I ever learnt was to always make friends with the engineer. Tell him what nice shoes he's got or offer to make some tea now and again. Then he'll explain what he's doing and why, and you'll learn – which is very important for survival.

"I hope you can get that far if that's what you want. It is possible. At school, the only music we had was a violin lesson. I wanted to join the music class, but they wouldn't let me 'cos they said I was tone-deaf! Cheers!"

PART TWO

HOW TO SET UP A LOCAL BREAKS FOR YOUNG BANDS CENTRE

Different Types of Breaks Centres

Part One went through how to get started in pop music; working with others; setting up a group; making demo tapes; promotion; getting gigs and making records without getting ripped off. This part of the book is about how to start a local Breaks For Young Bands Centre (whatever it happens to be called), how to keep it going, and how to make it grow.

At its simplest, a Breaks Centre could be just getting an unused or under-used room which you sound-proof for rehearsals by more than one young band. There could be a tape-recorder available for play-back and demo tapes.

A more elaborate Breaks Centre might be one or more sound-proofed rooms with a central store room for securing more sophisticated equipment. This would make possible the main purpose of a Breaks Centre – enabling young bands to:

■ **share, develop and improve musically**
■ **learn to maintain equipment**
■ **make demo discs and compilation records**
■ **understand how to make yourselves and your groups more effective and businesslike**

This type of Breaks Centre could be developed in an existing youth or community centre with the help of a full-time worker.

The most elaborate version of a Breaks Centre is one where young people from several bands club together to run it themselves, with or without the assistance of a youth or community worker. Such a Centre could be part of an existing community building or it might be a completely independent space.

73

Finding Other Groups

If you've followed the approach laid out in Part One, other young bands in your area should know who you are. It's likely, too, that you'll have a fair idea of who these other bands are and what they're doing.

If there's only one place for gigs in your area, you're likely to meet up with them there. You'll probably see them in the local record shop, or maybe in a particular bar or café, or down at the local arts centre.

There are thousands of young bands all over the country. They're all looking for places to rehearse, places to gig, and access to equipment, recording time, photocopying and printing. It's easier to join up and share the local resources than to compete for them.

In some areas the bands have joined up to form 'musicians collectives', or 'co-operatives'. This basically means that a number of bands decide to share certain things. For example, they've found that by sharing rehearsal space they can save money, because the space is being used all the time by a lot of groups.

Some of these collectives even hire out any spare equipment, book gigs and organize lessons together. Many of them have managed to get local council grants for sound-proofing material and recording equipment. Some of them have been able to record, press and distribute their own records.

Collectives like this are springing up all over Britain. Of course, some are more successful than others. They're not easy to run. You have to get the band members interested, not just in having free rehearsal space or getting things cheaper, but in helping run the operation. Then together you have to agree on rules that everyone will stick to.

If you're dealing with the Council, then you have to convince them you're serious. You also have to understand a bit about money, so that you can keep the thing running smoothly without going bust.

Bands are bound to be a bit competitive at first. You don't want your Breaks Centre to become an Argument Centre about who's the best band and who deserves the most rehearsal time. So if you have some organizers who aren't part of a band, they can help sort things out fairly without too much argument. This would be solved automatically in the case of setting up a Breaks Centre within a local youth, community or education centre which has staff who are willing to help.

As soon as you decide to start a Breaks Centre you run into a Catch 22 problem. You need two things – a place and a number of bands. But you can't get the bands without being able to offer them a place; and you can't convince anyone you need a place, if you haven't got the bands behind you wanting to use it.

So to begin with you have to check out a few things. Without actually promising anything definite, talk to other

people about the idea of setting up a Breaks Centre, especially the other local bands. The kind of answer you're looking for at this stage is something like 'If you get a place, we'll come in, as long as the deal is OK.'

Perhaps the most important thing you can do at this point is to speak to a few non-musicians. Find someone you think would be good at helping organize a local Breaks Centre. They might be youth workers, community workers or people from the local record or music shop. As mentioned above, the ideal person would be someone in charge of a local youth or community centre. If they're interested, they could sort out many of the practical problems listed above. Even if this happens, you'll still probably want to help organize and run the Breaks Centre with the other groups.

Finding Space

If you get this kind of support from the people you talk to, start looking for a useful space. You should turn back now and read pages 25 of this book 'Rehearsing and Rehearsal Rooms'. Go to the Council and ask for their list of empty buildings. Usually the Valuer's Department will have this and you have a right to see it. Some local councils have an Economic Development Unit or Employment Development Unit or Co-operative Development Agency which will have such a list. They might be able to help in other ways, with things like advice, loans or grants.

Start to sound people out – caretakers, neighbours, estate agents – anyone who might know if a certain building is empty, or has several empty rooms in it. Find out who owns it, and if there are any plans for it. Go and visit big public buildings in your area. Parts of them might be unused. Old buildings with thick walls are a good bet. If they're owned by the Council, the chances are they won't be able to sell them quickly.

If you find somewhere that looks promising, try asking the owner if you can bring some people round to have a look at it. If they ask why, say that you have an idea for a small business development – a music centre. Tell them that if others like the place you'll submit a proposal and a budget explaining what you're planning to do and what money is involved. Don't say you have more people involved than is really true.

In any case, it probably won't help as you're bound to get the usual objections about noise and vandalism. Be sure you're able to deal with these questions by talking about sound-proofing, putting down a deposit, and how you're going to have it very well organized. Also, you'll be better off dealing with these objections later, when you can show you mean business.

If you can't find an empty place, go to a local youth club and tell the worker there what you'd like to do. Ask him or her to help you find a place.

Finding Other Help

Once you've seen a place that's possible, you need to start thinking about getting together a number of people who can help the Centre. It's not just musicians you're looking for. You'll want technicians, electricians, and sound engineers who can record, fix broken gear, and build up equipment cheaply from components. You might also want graphic artists who can set up photographic, printing and silkscreening facilities for artwork, posters and sleeves.

Someone interested in business or a youth worker might be able to show you how to look after the money in the early stages. They might put time in to supervise and help. Why not try the local Rotary Club? Perhaps your local Enterprise Agency might help. They are listed in the telephone directory. In other words, you want anyone who's interested and capable, to help organize and publicize what you're doing.

So, when you've got a few people together and have a space in mind, you might want to have a public meeting. Run off some posters saying why, when and where you're meeting, and listing the sort of people you're looking for.

For instance:

Breaks
for young Bands
Centre

YOUNG MUSICIANS, TECHNICIANS AND ARTISTS OF GREAT SNORING.

WANT A REHEARSAL AND RECORDING CENTRE? JOIN US TO TRY TO GET ONE.

Monday night, 35 April, at the Stuffed Pigeon

Tel: 123-4567.

Cover the area with posters (see page 49) and go round in person chatting it up in local record shops, discos, youth clubs, art centres, and in the street. Write down people's names and phone numbers if they show real interest. Explain what you're doing and have some photocopied handouts you can give people to read. But remember, it's word of mouth that sells, not posters or bits of paper left lying around. Those just act as reminders.

If you campaign enthusiastically and do a telephone chase-up before the meeting, you should get a fair turnout. Explain to them what you want to do and the sort of help you're looking for. Tell them what they can get out of it and what they'll have to put in if they join a collective of bands or an association to set up a Breaks Centre. Tell people you need to show that there's a big demand to stand a chance of getting the place and the funding together.

Stress the give-and-take aspect – everyone has to help with some of the decorating, sound-proofing, engineering or organizing. If they do, they can get a share of the rehearsal and recording time at member's rates when the place is ready. Suggest the idea of pooling equipment, both for recording and for gigging. Also suggest hiring out equipment to get some funds into the kitty.

Some people will probably show no interest. Some will prick up their ears at the possibility of cheap rehearsal and recording time. Others will be genuinely interested in the possibility of setting up a Breaks Centre. Ask them their ideas about solving any of the problems you're facing.

Say that you're going to call another meeting for those who are really interested after you get the support of the authorities or others for a Breaks Centre. You should ask for some volunteers for a temporary working group to help you get this support.

Now that you have several groups and individuals interested, you have a power base. Say you have five. groups and ten other individuals. That's likely to be about thirty-five people. Thirty-five people who are organized and committed are an army. If you each put in £1.00 a week, or even 50p, you would probably be able to get hold of a small space and pay for all the costs to run it. There are many other ways to pay for this as you'll see by reading on.

Setting It Up

Once you've got your eye on a building and have some other people involved, your next task should be to figure out the money angle.

There will be two sets of figures: Set-Up Costs and Running Costs.

Set-Up Costs How much will it cost to fix up, decorate and sound-proof? Does it need rewiring? How much equipment do you need to start? (Remember, you can always add more later.) How much furniture will you need? Do you have to pay a deposit or a premium to get hold of the place?

The way to go about answering these questions is to make a list of everything from paint and paint-brushes to speakers and mikes. Then go out and see what the things cost new and what they cost second-hand. (See the short sample price-list, 'What's the Damage?', page 114)

Next, see what equipment the bands who want to share already have, and what you can borrow. Tell them you're going to insure everything. Find out from an insurance broker what the cost might be. Don't be afraid of ringing an insurance broker. They make their money from putting together the best deal for you and they get their payment from the insurance companies.

Now you'll know what's left to get and how much it might cost to set up a Breaks Centre.

Running Costs

There's no point in going after the things you need to set up the Breaks Centre, until you know:

- ■ **how much it's going to cost to run it**
- ■ **how you're going to pay for it**
- ■ **how big it is**

The questions you have to ask about regular weekly, monthly or annual costs are:

- ■ **How much rent will there be?**
- ■ **What will the rates be?**
- ■ **What will heating and electricity cost?**
- ■ **What will the costs be for repairs, new windows, light-bulbs, etc?**
- ■ **What will insurance cost? (You should have obtained this figure from an insurance broker.)**
- ■ **Do you have to pay for staff, caretakers, or security? If so, how much?**
- ■ **What does it cost for different kinds of phones?**
- ■ **Are there any hidden costs?**

This may seem like you're down and out before you're up and running. Don't worry. Each of these things can be dealt with, but you have to think it through, one step at a time. If you don't, then the whole project will come to a sticky end, and you may be stuck with large bills.

Let's look at each one of the things listed under the heading of 'Running Costs'.

Rent If you're in a public building or using part of one, you should be able to use the place free. Or you might get a licence for £1.00 a year. (That's called a 'peppercorn rent'; it means a legal deal has been made for next to nothing.)

Rates The same thing should be true of rates as for rent if you're in a public building; that is, you probably won't have to pay them. If you're in a place on your own and not part of someone else's centre, then there's a way to lower the rates bill. Work through a local charity.

Charities only have to pay half-rates. Councils can also decide to let a charity off paying the other half of the rates. So by becoming a charity or by working through one, you could end up not paying rates at all.

To find a suitable local charity to work with, go and ask the Citizens' Advice Bureau or local arts centre or your Council for Voluntary Service (CVS). You'll find them listed in the telephone directory.

Heating and Electricity If you're in a public building that someone else is running, you may not have to pay for heating and electricity. The way to find out what they cost is to go to the Electricity Board and ask them to help. Or go to a heating consultant. Or ask the Council's Architects Department to help you.

For them to be able to help you, in any of these cases, you'll need to know:

- the amount of floor space
- how high the ceilings are
- how many light points there are
- how many pieces of equipment of how many watts you will have on
- for how many hours a day you will use each of these things

Repairs You'll probably find the cost of this difficult even to guess at. The best way to deal with this might be to make an agreement. It might say that all bulbs and repairs on commonly used things will be paid for equally by each band in your collective.

One good way to handle this is to set up a central fund which your fund-raising events, or dues, or charges get paid into. Even if you need this money for other things, you should try hard to keep part of it to pay for these things. When a bulb or fuse blows in the middle of recording, you don't want to have an argument or call a meeting to decide who has to pay for it.

Insurance If you're in a public building, ask the people running it if you're covered by their insurance. The chances are you will be. If not, then you ought to have insurance for fire, theft, and for the people using the building, in case they get hurt. This is called Third-Party insurance.

If the building is yours, you'll want to insure it as well. If your equipment isn't covered, you should look into this. As mentioned before, go to an insurance broker and ask. In order to qualify for insurance on equipment, you have to show that it's kept in a secure lock-up space. The better the security, the more they like it. Make sure you have good padlocks and barred windows.

Staff If you are in a collective that's just starting up, then you'll be taking turns doing certain jobs like cleaning, locking up, keeping the place repaired, answering the phone, keeping the books, and sorting out the schedules for using everything.

If there's a full-time use of your Breaks Centre, you're going to need a full-time person looking after the place for reasons of security, sorting out problems, meeting guests and so on. Whoever it is, everyone has to agree what their job and responsibilities are. It doesn't matter what title they have; for now, just call this role the 'gaffer'.

Telephone It might be a good idea at first to put in a coin-box phone. This should have an extra padlocked security bar across it to stop break-ins. Put it where it can be seen by lots of people. Make sure that British Telecom block it from being able to accept collect calls. This is a common way that people try to rip off public coin-box telephones.

If you have a coin box at first, at least you can be sure to pay the phone bills including the rental charge. You may even make a bit of money from it. Later, if you install an office phone, you'll have to set a rule about who can use it. It's probably best to keep the coin box as well for everyone's personal calls.

There are at least eight ways to get the money you need. But remember it's the things that you want; raising money is only one way to get them.

1 Everyone or each group can put in a share of the cash needed. If you don't have any savings, why not decide to take odd jobs or part-time jobs together, and put the money in the kitty.

There's a good model for setting up odd-job co-operatives, called Instant Muscle, which can earn money in this way. You might want to buy the handbook on setting up one of these. You can find where to get it on page 122 at the back of this book. You could even use this model for your collective to set up and run your Breaks Centre.

2 The Breaks Centre or the members of the collective, should be able to earn a lot of its own costs. Hiring out the rooms and equipment, even at a low price, will add up. You'll probably think of a lot of other ways to keep the costs down and other ways for the Breaks Centre to earn its keep.

3 Ask local businesses or the manufacturers to donate the things you need. Tell them you don't need them new or in perfect condition, just usable.

4 The collective can do a sponsored event. See if the local radio station will help. You could try to get into the *Guinness Book of Records* by playing the longest ever session. You might be able to do this in the window of the local music shop, if it's big enough. It might bring them some business. Or you might set a record for playing all of the Beatles' songs with your toes.

5 You might be able to get a grant from a charitable trust, a business association, the Council, or the Regional Arts Association. You can get advice on how to contact these agencies from your Local Council for Voluntary Service. Also there are many addresses listed at the back of this book. Find out the names and addresses of the managers of the most successful bands, especially ones originally from your area. Write to them asking if they have set up a charitable trust, and if so, could they help you.

6 If any of those you apply to won't give you a grant, ask them if they'll give you an interest-free loan. Before you do this, make sure you've worked out how you'll repay it.

7 If you're going to fit your Breaks Centre into a youth centre of half-used adult education centre or whatever, the people running these places may have budgets to do repairs and renovations.

8 You could ask the local paper or radio station to do a feature asking for donations of equipment or instruments. Put up notices in all likely places asking for these as well.

Finally, remember that no one will help you unless you really set up to help young bands get a break. No matter which or how many of the other ways you choose to raise funds or get resources given, it's a good idea to do numbers one and two above as well. If each band or individual has put in an equal sum, then you know they're serious and so does everyone else.

To put everything written above in a nutshell, your best chance is to try to get a space in a public or charitable building like a youth club, adult education centre, or an arts or community centre. If it has staff who are interested, then you've got it made.

If you can't, you'll have to find a building or space to fix up and run yourselves. Then you'll have to go through it step by step to find out if you can meet the costs either by everyone paying an equal share for equal use or through other earnings. If you still can't meet the bills, then you may have to apply for a grant.

There are a number of organizations, private and public, which can give money to musicians' collectives: charitable trusts, borough councils, local arts councils, regional arts associations, small business schemes, and the Department of the Environment's Urban Programme which you apply to through your local council. Just because you get a 'no' from one of them doesn't mean you shouldn't try all the others.

If you are going to apply for a grant you should put in your applications quickly to the Council or to trusts for two reasons. In the first place, the answer you get might make a big difference to the size of your Breaks Centre. The second reason is that it will probably take several months to get a reply.

If you wait to apply, you may well find you have everything else sorted out except the possibility of a grant. This will mean twiddling your thumbs instead of the recording dials. You might also lose your chance to get hold of the building or space.

There are lots of places to get help from and it takes a lot of work to go through them all. On the other hand, this means that there are a lot of chances to succeed. On page 115 here's a list of many of the bodies worth approaching, and what each of them deals with. It doesn't list well-known bands, which you can track down yourself. But remember to keep a copy of each letter you write.

Convincing People

Even when you find a disused space which would be perfect for rehearsing and recording in, you've probably still got the hardest part ahead of you. This is convincing whoever's in charge of the space that you should be allowed to use it. Youth workers and people running arts or community centres will tend to be the most sympathetic. But remember, they don't have the final say.

You know you won't disturb anyone or damage the property. You're willing to swear to this on your holy instrument. Yet some people may still take a lot of persuading to let you set up. Even if you agree to pay rent, they might still refuse. If they're caretaker-managers or Council employees, they'll be worried about complaints from their bosses: 'What! You let our empty storage space out to a gang of punks?'

These people might make a lot of silly objections like 'You'll spill your hair dye on the floor,' or 'You look strange so you'll probably act strange.' It's important not to get annoyed or frustrated with them. After all, you probably have the same type of prejudice about them: 'They dress straight, so they're probably creeps.'

Usually they just want to make sure they have all the answers, even the ones to stupid questions, so that they can answer their bosses. They don't necessarily want to keep you out. They probably just don't want to lose their jobs or get taken for a ride, which is fair enough.

Whether the space you find is Council property or privately owned, the only way in is to show that you're business-like. You have to assume that people are going to think that you're a gang of noisy hooligans unless you can prove otherwise. So show them that you've thought about it. Explain to them clearly, one point at a time, exactly what you intend to do with the space. Show them you've thought about security, cleaning the place, paying the bills and not disturbing the neighbours.

One interesting way to get a space has come up

recently. For the past few years private businesses and local councils have been setting up workshop buildings to help small businesses setup. Over 90 per cent of metropolitan councils have been doing this. In the past, most of these workshops have been in new buildings.

Now some councils are starting to think about renovating old buildings for this kind of use. If you really have your act together, you might persuade your council to let you do one of these. A Breaks Centre is different from the usual thing in this field, but so what? It's worth a try.

License or Lease

One good way to get hold of a space is to ask for a licence instead of a lease. Under the law, a lease is usually for several years; and you have the right to stay there no matter what, so long as you pay your rent and don't break the law. But a licence is for a limited period of time. You have to promise to get out, say, in a year or two. Also, these deals usually only require you to pay a very small amount to use the space.

What's good about a licence is:

> ■ you don't have to agree to pay rent for several years
> ■ you get a chance to see if the project is going to work
> ■ the owner, usually the Council, feels much better about this because you'll promise to leave if they need the building
> ■ you have to pay only a small amount to use the building each year

What's bad about a licence is:

> ■ you might have to leave when the time's up even if you're making a go of it.

There are two ways around this. First, see if you can get them to agree in writing to rehouse you if they need the space back. Also see if they'll agree to pay you for the re-fitting you did so you can do this to the new place. Second, try to get them to agree to renew the licence for a year at a time if the project's going well and if they don't need the space.

Remember, you must leave the building at the end of the licence if you've promised you will. But, if by then you've made a go of your Breaks Centre, you're likely to have little trouble finding another space – probably a much better one.

After you list your set-up costs (page 81) and your running costs (page 82), show how much money you plan to earn each week from hiring out rehearsal space, recording time, instruments and PA systems; how much from using the space as a teaching centre; and perhaps even how much from your own pockets from earnings.

If you can balance your running costs with your earnings, then the Breaks Centre makes sense as a business. It would be a non-commercial business, but it's still a business. If this is the case, you'll stand a much better chance of getting hold of a space and finding the money and equipment to set it up. The reasons for this are that you won't need a grant, you won't have to wait around, you'll be able to decide things for yourselves, and you'll still be able to pay all your bills.

The best way to explain all these things is to write a short proposal. You'll need this anyway to apply for a grant. It doesn't have to be more than a couple of pages, plus your Setting-Up and Running Costs budgets. The proposal should explain who's doing it, what the Breaks Centre is going to be used for, who will use it, a sample weekly schedule, and how it's going to work financially. Try to get it typed up neatly.

It may be a good idea to consult a community worker or your local Enterprise Agency to help you sort this out and present it. Other people who might be able to help you are listed at the back of this book, on page 120. Remember, these people are paid to help others set things up. Ask them for advice and help.

Private Meeting

By now you have met with (written to or phoned) local councillors and officers, estate agents, caretakers, landlords, music officers from the Regional Arts Association, youth and community workers, local business people, people who give grants, and other advisers.

This might be the time to get together with everyone who is in a position to help you. There may be one or two key people who aren't sold yet on the idea that they should help. Invite them too, but just a few of this type at most. They'll be convinced by all the others who support you.

Also, by now you'll have found at least one person who seems very interested and who can help. This might be your ward councillor or a local youth and community worker. Work with them to set up this private meeting. Write down the people whose help is important to you to set up the Breaks Centre. List them, starting with the most important. Ring the top five (via their secretaries) and see which date and times they might have free.

Once you've got a meeting time which most people can make, send out an invitation to everyone on your list.

Tell them the following:

- **how long the meeting will last; say one hour**
- **what it's for: to sort out problems with, and the next step for, the Breaks For Young Bands Centre**
- **who has already agreed to come: the Mayor, your Ward Councillor, etc.**

You might be able to get the Mayor to chair this meeting. The job of mayors is to do things like this; but they're very busy and booked up long in advance. Every Mayor is an elected local Councillor. They get the year off from other Council duties to go around meeting groups, opening things, and being the spokesperson for your town. If you can't get the Mayor, then perhaps you could ask the Senior Youth Officer in your district.

You should get the bands and others who want to be in the collective to elect three or four delegates to go to this meeting. Probably you should all agree in advance that just one of you will be the spokesperson. This meeting is different from your public meeting. At this meeting you want to get to people to help. Get them to decide what they can do to sort out any problems you still have. Make sure you meet the person who is chairing the meeting beforehand and go over everything with him or her.

Remember your goal for this meeting is to get everyone's support for your Breaks Centre. Try to get everyone there to agree to do something when they leave the meeting. Then make sure you follow up their promises.

Remember, they're all busy people and they have other equally important things to do. It's your Breaks Centre. You have to remind them and prove you mean business. You've got to supply the energy and the pressure without becoming a nuisance.

If you haven't asked them already to become advisers, do so at the meeting. If there are people there you don't want as advisers, then ask those you do want privately, after the meeting. Tell them you'd like to list their names on your stationery.

Stationery

A nother way to appear business-like is to have your own stationery properly printed. It's cheap to do and it helps convince people you're serious. Things that people look for when they get a letter are credentials, people's names, sponsors and where to reply.

You can use Letraset and a typewriter to do your own master, then photocopy or duplicate it. If you've found some designers, one of them will do the artwork for a letterhead for you. It would look even better if you went to one of the new High Street printshops. They sometimes do all the work for stationery very cheaply.

As mentioned earlier, one good thing to do is to get some of the people who have been advising you to agree to have their names listed as 'Advisers'. If you haven't asked them at your meetings, then write to them to get their agreement.

Tell them they won't have to come to regular meetings; it won't cost them anything; they won't have any financial responsibility for the Breaks Centre if it fails; and it won't take much time. Tell them what you would really like from them is advice when you need it and for them to help you with contacts.

The same thing can be true for 'Patrons'. You might be able to get some well-known rock-stars to lend you their names as Patrons. You might think of other very well-known local people whose names would be impressive. Promise them the same thing as for the Advisers.

People are very good about helping in this way if they know you're not after their money or time. Everyone likes to think you want them for themselves, their brains and who they are. Don't you feel the same way? Who knows, you might end up with them giving you a bit of their time for an appearance and an occasional donation. Let them decide this for themselves though.

Also, you'll want to put at the bottom of the stationery a line saying what kind of organization you are. If you haven't finally registered (see page 98), just say you're doing it. It's like when the tax disc on a car has run out and the owner puts up a notice saying 'tax in post'.

When you write letters on this stationery, try to use a typewriter. Otherwise write very neatly and clearly, using correct spelling and writing properly. This is a good way to impress those whose help you need with how business-like you are. But don't worry if it's not perfect. What counts is that you're doing it yourself and that you've taken the trouble to do it as well as you can.

See the illustration of the stationery for examples of all of these things.

NAME OF YOUR CITY OR TOWN
Breaks for young Bands Centre
c/o Address: Phone Number
A Music Centre for Self-Help By The Young People of Great Snoring

Advisers:
Committee:
Patrons:
The Great Snoring Breaks For Young Bands Centre is being registered as a not-for-profit company with charitable objectives to house the Musictown's Musicians' Collective.

Constitution

Notice the line at the bottom of the stationery: 'The Great Snoring Breaks For Young Bands Centre is being registered as a not-for-profit company with charitable objectives to house the Musictown's Collective.'

Obviously you won't write this, but you should write in something that says what kind of organization you are. This means, of course, you have to decide on a basic set of rules – a constitution – that you're going to use. This is a formality, but it's a very important one.

Without it you won't be able to:

- ■ **open a bank account in the name of the Breaks Centre**
- ■ **get grants from the Council or from trusts**
- ■ **sort out what happens if everything goes wrong without a lot of legal hassles**
- ■ **avoid paying off the debts yourselves personally if it does all go wrong**

Even if you do have a proper constitution you still might have to pay off the debts. This would happen if the people you owe money to decided to take you to court; and they prove that you didn't try to run the Breaks Centre with the proper care and attention.

It's quite simple to vote on and adopt a constitution. You don't have to write one up from scratch. You simply have to have a meeting to agree to this basic set of rules. A constitution is usually written in formal language because it's a legal document. Quite a straightforward and short one is printed at the back of the book on page 124.

This one sets up a local association. You can call it what you like. The example at the back is called 'Breaks For Young Bands Association of Your Town'.

There are two very good kinds of legal structures for a Breaks Centre. One is an 'association' which is what a collective is anyway.

The other is a 'company limited by guarantee'. This is a not-for-profit company. You would only want to set up this legal structure if you had a lot of property and equipment. The constitution of such a company is called its 'articles and memorandum of association'.

If you want to set up this type, you need specialist legal advice. You can get it from a local solicitor who might do it free except for the registration charge. This costs about £100. Or you can get help to do this from your local Council for Voluntary Service, or from Inter-Action Centre Ltd, or NCVO. The addresses of the last two are listed at the back of this book.

The sample constitution for an association is written so that it can be registered as a charity with the Charity Commissioners in London and with the Board of Inland Revenue. Being a charity gives the organization the benefits of at least half off the rates, no business taxes and the right to apply for and to receive charitable donations untaxed.

There are a few basic things that can't be changed in a charity. One is the list of objects (or purposes or reasons) you give for why you're doing it. The wording of the objects clause in the example at the back has already been judged to be charitable by the Charity Commission and Inland Revenue.

Another thing you can't do is divide up the property or income of the charity amongst the members personally.

If you want to try to become a charity, now or in the future, then don't touch the objects clause (no. 2), the amendment clause (no. 10) and the dissolution or winding-up clause (no. 12) given in the sample. If you don't want to be a charity, then change these as you think best.

In any case, you can change all of the other clauses to suit yourselves. Make sure in doing this that you still keep practical and sensible rules for sorting out problems, rules for voting, keeping accounts, minutes and so on.

Sometimes people get confused and start arguing about every word in a constitution when they're trying to set it up. They don't realize that a constitution isn't the rule-book for the day-to-day running of things. It's simply a set of general common-sense rules for the fair setting up of the game, like the numbers of players on a football team, the size of the pitch and where the goal-mouth is. These are the things that are commonly accepted.

What you really want to spend your time discussing is how you're going to play the game each day. This is a separate set of day-to-day rules (called 'bye-laws' or 'house rules') which you can change whenever you find it necessary.

The way the constitution and house rules connect is that you can't make a house rule that steps out of the boundary of the constitution. You wouldn't allow the goalkeeper to turn the goal-mouth around facing the stands behind, would you? Where the goal-mouth is located, its size, shape and direction, are fixed rules (constitutional). How you defend your goal is a changing set of rules and tactics (house rules).

Follow-Up Meeting

By now you've held your meeting with advisers and others, – the private meeting. Or you have the support of some advisers and other people with access to buildings. The time has come to hold a follow-up meeting. Remember? You promised this at your first public meeting with the bands and individuals who want to be in the collective. You probably have kept in touch with them anyway through your temporary working group or through bumping into them in clubs and cafés.

Before you call the follow-up meeting, prepare for it. Get the working group and others to agree a form of a constitution to be voted on at the meeting. It would be simplest just to adopt something like the sample one at the back. You have to discuss how you fill in the blanks for the association's name, ages of members and things like that.

At the meeting, explain why you need a formal constitution and what each thing means. Also explain that the

house rules will be the real day-to-day system. This will be worked out together when you get your space. Let people make suggestions. Listen carefully and then vote on everything.

After voting for the Constitution, have each group put forward the name of a representative for election to the committee. Let any other individual who wants to be on the committee have the chance to stand for election.

Make sure your committee is not so large that you won't be able to get things done. More than about sixteen members might prove unworkable. Remember you can set up sub-committees or working groups to try to sort out particular things, like catering or a compilation record or decorating.

End the meeting by making sure you have everyone's name, address and phone number and that they know how to contact the committee.

Now that you have your committee, have them elect a chairperson, secretary, treasurer and other officers you all think you need.

If you plan your meeting well, you could do all the following in about an hour:

- **Vote for the proposed constitution**
- **Elect a committee**
- **End the public meeting**
- **Hold a committee meeting to elect the officers**
- **Sign the constitution**

Later the secretary will write up the minutes of the two meetings.

Now you can go to a bank to open an account in the name of the association. They'll give you a mandate form which you fill in and return with your constitution attached.

You're also now ready to do all of the other things necessary – from getting a building or space in someone else's building, to applying for grants, collecting together equipment and so on.

Even if your proposal is accepted by landlords and donors, and if you're able to set up a Breaks Centre, or fit into an existing Centre, you still have another job to do. You've convinced people outside the collective that you mean business, and the collective has become an association.

Now you've got to convince the collective itself to work hard and together. This is a crucial stage, as any mistakes you make at this point will be hard to correct later. This is the stage where you have to set up a system – the set of house rules that everyone agrees to stick to. Setting up of these house rules might be another occasion when it's helpful to have a community worker or youth worker present.

Your collective has agreed to a constitution. That means you have the legal structure needed to back you up.

House Rules

Now the Committee has to agree on the real nitty-gritty of how the Breaks Centre is actually going to run. Make sure you're thinking about a real space and real problems. Don't just imagine what it might be like. You should hold off on your house rules until you have a house!

But once the committee has agreed on everything you can think of for the time being, then put it all down in writing. These are your house rules or bye-laws. Then call a General Meeting of everyone who wants to become involved. Get everyone to sign these house rules. Now any argument in future can be solved by pointing to these house rules as agreed and as set down in black and white.

The following points should all be cleared up in your house rules:

Money

- **Where and how should it be kept?**
- **Who is allowed to take it out?**
- **Who decides what to spend it on?**
- **What counts as a private expense and what as a collective expense?**
- **Do all the different operations – recording, studio, PA hire, printing, etc – pool their money, or do they earn and spend independently?**

Time

- **How much rehearsal and recording time does each group have?**
- **How much do members pay and how much for non-members?**
- **Who decides which band has first choice?**
- **What happens with cancellations?**
- **When does the gaffer have to be there?**

Gear

■ **Whose responsibility is it?**
■ **Who mends broken equipment?**
■ **Who pays for it: the Centre, or the person who broke it?**
■ **Who has first claim on it?**
■ **What are the rules about using recording tape?**
■ **What are the rules about wiping over old tape?**
■ **How is tape logged and stored?**

Collectives around the country have found out the hard way. These points must all be sorted out at the beginning. Unless you do this, there is no way of sorting out all the answers when they come up without having a big bust-up. Also everything should be as open and as above-board as possible.

The house rules should be displayed on a notice-board. The charges for use of rooms, tape, equipment and all other things should also be on a notice-board.

There should be weekly schedules stating clearly:

■ **who is rehearsing/recording**
■ **from when till when**
■ **with what equipment**

Everyone should be clear about who is responsible for each session.

This may sound very strict. But it's the only way to make sure that the space, time and money you have are all going to be used as fairly and efficiently as possible. You want to get on with your music, not with arguments. Without planning, and without clearly stating fair policies, the shared use of any building or equipment turns into a big hassle.

104

Developing It

Once you've started up a collective and a Breaks Centre, there are any number of ways it might develop. You may find a space large enough to hold gigs in. This might become the local music venue with rehearsal space and a small recording studio attached.

You may find you have a team so good at fixing equipment that you can advertise and become a repair centre. You might get a grant from the local Council or Regional Arts Association for the whole project. Or at least a grant might pay for your rent or perhaps even for staf and some running costs.

'Livewire' is a movement supported by organizations that give advice and financial help to young people who are setting up projects and businesses. If you do a good job in getting your collective off the ground, you might qualify for an award. This could mean up to a £1000 award for your Breaks Centre! There may be a Livewire contact in your area; see page 121 for addresses.

If you have a big building and your lease or licence allows you to sub-let, you might like to think about making some money for the association. You might be able to move a commercial business into your building to pay rent to you. They would have to pay rates as well.

These wouldn't be just any old businesses, but ones that would make sense to have next to you, like a hairdresser, a poster shop or a record shop. In other words, if you really have a hundred or more young people a day coming to the Breaks Centre, isn't it a good location for the kinds of businesses that want you all as their customers?

Jobs

Getting all the jobs done of cleaning, security, scheduling, book-keeping, etc. is the most difficult part of any collective. The jobs themselves aren't so difficult. The problem is chasing people to do them. Seeing that everyone does what they said they would do – on time and properly – is the real back-breaker. Others have done it though, so you can too.

Some tips:

1 Always have two people assigned to each job. One can be a back-up in case of sickness, holidays, etc. It's also easier to face a job if someone else is helping. You can learn from each other and moan to each other.

2 Get groups or individuals to sign a piece of paper saying what they promise to do. This could be called their job-description.

3 Put out a schedule for jobs each week on the central notice-board. Also hand out printed copies listing who's in charge, what they have to do, and when they have to do it.

4 Have a blackboard next to the notice-board so you can put up 'stop press' news or changes. Everyone will know to look at this and you won't have to call meetings all the time when things come up.

5 Have your weekly committee meeting to make changes and to agree the assignments, but not to do making up the list. It could take forever. Have one person sort out the list beforehand for the committee to vote on.

6 Have a fortnightly or monthly meeting of everybody (not just the committee) to discuss problems and ideas. Make sure you have a regular time and that you make a list of things that need to be discussed. Put it on the blackboard.

7 Maybe you could work it so that anyone who wants to have something discussed can do this too. They just add their thing to the agenda, for the committee meeting, or the full meeting on the blackboard whenever they think of it.

8 Make sure you always have a gaffer looking after the place someone who has everyone's agreement to be in charge at that time. It can't be someone who is rehearsing or recording.

9 Make sure you keep a record of the decisions made at all meetings. The Secretary usually does this. These minutes should all be entered into the Minute Book. A copy of the minutes of each meeting should be put up on the notice-board the next day, if possible.

10 Watch out for the ego-trippers who want everything, but aren't willing to do their share. If you find people being unfair in this way, the committee has the right, according to the Constitution, to stop their membership.

This may all sound bureaucratic, but it isn't. It's democratic and good common-sense. Unless everyone knows what's happening and what's been decided, you'll have misunderstandings, rows and a bust-up. There are two main reasons for collectives failing, and money isn't one of them! The two are – not keeping records clearly and openly; and the trouble caused by ego-trippers.

Money and Things

Of course money is one of the things which will decide whether you succeed or fail: earning or finding money on the one hand; and on the other hand, figuring out how to replace actual cash with your ideas, energy and labour. Remember, it's the things you need the money for, not money for its own sake. Sometimes businesses find it much easier to give you shopworn demonstration equipment or even new stuff rather than cash. People can often put in time free, but not money.

It should be clear by now that you have to keep track of every penny. The reason for this is not simply because it's good business practice. There are nasty and envious people around who will accuse the committee of ripping off the collective. Properly kept books, open to everyone, will shut up these troublemakers.

From the very earliest stage onwards, there must be someone on the committee, the Treasurer, who automatically keeps track of all the money that comes in and goes out. He or she also has to put down where, when, who got it and how it went out. This doesn't require a whizz-kid, but it does need to be done regularly and clearly.

All you need is someone who's honest and good with figures. They have to sit down for a few minutes each day and be accurate about writing it all down. Your Treasurer may need to chat to a community or a businessperson or Council accountant early on, to be told what books to keep.

After that, the treasurer will be the person who knows exactly how much money you should have, how much you are owed and where it is. Also make sure everyone knows where the accounts are kept and how to understand them. Go and look at them occasionally. In this way, the group as a whole keeps control of the project. Have the Treasurer give you all a report at your weekly meeting.

You might be able to find someone from the Chamber of Commerce or an arts centre or the Rotary Club who will act as an adviser on this part.

Cash Flow

There's more to keeping track of money than meets the eye. Of course you can't have more money flowing out than you have flowing in, or you're broke. But if you spend money before you've paid the amount to cover it, you'll be broke too. Even profitable jobs can bankrupt you!

For example, say you've been offered £200 to fix some equipment. You could do with the cash, because you've only got £30 in the collective account. What's more, the replacement parts only cost £80, so you stand to clear £120 for your labour. But actually, you can't really afford to do the job, because you haven't got the £80 to buy the parts. You need £50 more.

That's an example of a profitable job you can't afford unless you came up with the £50 you need by everyone chipping in. You could try talking to the bank, friends or family about a loan. This problem is called cash flow and everybody has it. It's like wanting to go to a concert on Thursday night, but you don't get paid until Friday. One way to solve this is to ask the customer about paying you some of the money up front. Try to make sure that everyone who will owe you money pays in advance. At least make sure they pay on time.

Depreciation

Here's another thing to remember: all the gear is worth less each time you use it. It's depreciating. This is another reason why you can't spend as much as you bring in. If you buy an amp for £50, then in six months' time you'll be lucky to get £40 for it. So some of the money you make out of hiring gear has to be put aside for replacing stuff that's slowly wearing out or just getting out of date.

The Treasurer should keep in mind the question of how much it's going to cost to replace the gear, like the £50 amp, compared to how much you'd actually get if you sold it. Then you've got to keep enough money saved up to cover the difference, like the tenner in the case of the amp.

Compilation Albums

If you come out ahead with your money though – if you get a grant or sponsorship, or make money out of the Breaks Centre – you have to decide how to spend it. If you've adopted a charitable constitution, then you can't share out the cash to yourselves. One thing you could do is to move to a bigger or better space. Or you could buy more equipment. One really good investment for all concerned is to make an album early on.

A number of collectives have put out compilation albums featuring all the bands who rehearse or play in their Breaks Centre. These albums are almost always successful. They cost less than you think. If every member of every group on the album makes an effort to sell copies to all their friends and relatives, and at their gigs, it's quite possible to sell out a pressing of 1000 copies pretty quickly.

The Inter-Action organization has set up something called Make-It-Yourself which shows how groups can make and sell their own records with a very small investment. Their address is on page 115.

As well as making a small surplus, or at least breaking even, having a record out can do a number of good things.

First of all, every band gets some prestige from having a vinyl recording out in a nice sleeve. It always looks much more professional than a demo tape. This is one good reason for a band to join a collective in the first place. But if it's the only reason, then they're probably not going to be very helpful or co-operative members.

Some Breaks Centres have been started as agencies where the organizer or association takes 10 per cent of all the bands giving them gig money in return for a guarantee of a track on a compilation album. This is a way of starting a collective without having a centre or any shared rehearsal space.

Secondly, it makes the collective more professional. It gives everyone – the musicians, the engineers, the sleeve designers – a chance to produce something which looks good and sounds good. You can show it and play it to anyone with pride. You may find that people take you much more seriously once you've got an album out. You may also find it easier to get money for other projects. In that sense a record can be a very good investment.

Also, a record will help you communicate with other collectives around the country. Quite a few now have albums out which means you can listen to each other's music. This might lead to linking up for rehearsals, gigs or festivals.

All of this emphasis on producing a compilation record shouldn't mislead you though. The main reasons for joining together to try to set up a Breaks Centre have to do with learning with and from others, being with people who share your interests, and trying to run things as much as possible by yourselves democratically.

You may eventually find that you've learned a lot and you've helped a lot of other people in addition to yourselves. You'll be playing an important role in a growing organization. In short, you'll have done the most creative thing there is – making something out of nothing.

Glossary

AMP (Amplifier)
A piece of electrical gear that boosts the tiny electrical signal which comes out of electric instruments into enough power to drive a loudspeaker.

Combo
An amplifier and loudspeaker 'combined' in one portable unit.

Bass-bin
Loudspeaker designed to reproduce lower-frequency sounds.

Crossover
This bit of electrical gear splits the output from the power amp into 3 frequency ranges: bass, middle and treble. These signals are then connected to the right speakers for each frequency.

Flightcase
A sturdy case, often made of aluminium, which protects equipment from being bashed.

Four-track
A reel-to-reel or cassette tape recorder which allows you to record on four separate channels or tracks.

Horns
A loudspeaker designed to reproduce high frequency sounds as part of a PA system.

Impedance
The outputs of electrical instruments and the outputs and inputs of amplifiers are given an impedance value. This is measured in 'OHMS' and is indicated by a number followed by the symbol "Ω" like this 600 Ω . To get the best performance from your gear, it's important to match the impedance values especially for speakers.

Mid-bin
A loudspeaker designed to reproduce sounds in the mid-frequency range as part of PA system.

Mixer
The box with all the knobs on'. A mixer is used to balance the volume and sound of each instrument or voice in a band so that together they make a good sound. The person who operates the mixer is also called the 'mixer'.

Monitor
A small loudspeaker placed in front of musicians on stage so that members of the band can hear their own sound.

Multicore
Thick cable, often with thirty smaller cables inside it; used to connect all the gear on stage to the mixer.

PA Gear
(Public Address Equipment) The extra gear needed by a band, in addition to amps they're using, to make themselves heard well enough in a large hall or venue. The PA set-up includes bass-bins, mid-bins, horns, a power amp, stage box, mixer and multicore, monitors and a crossover.

Portastudio
A 4-track cassette recorder and mixer combined in one portable unit.

Power Amp
A powerful amplifier which is used to drive the 3 sorts of speaker in a PA system.

Soundcheck
A few numbers played before the gig to allow the mixer to set the controls on the mixing desk to the correct levels.

Stagebox
A box on stage into which all the band's microphones are plugged. A multicore cable then connects the stage box to the mixer.

Appendices:

Whats the Damage

This is a very rough guide to some typical prices for fairly standard equipment. Obviously these prices will vary from region to region. You might get better bargains second-hand than those listed. In any case, this is how much it cost to get a band going in the summer of '84.

INSTRUMENTS	NEW	SECOND-HAND
Acoustic guitar	£40–150	£25–100
Electric guitar	£100+	£50–200
Bass guitar	£100+	£50–100
Electric piano	£200–400	£80–100
Saxophone	£320+	£200–250
Flute	£150+	£80–120
Drum machine	£100+	£75–150
Drums (bass, snare and hi-hat)	£200+	£80–150

PA AND RECORDING GEAR	HIRE (per day)	NEW	SECOND-HAND
4-Track Reel-to-Reel	£20	£800	£450–550
Portastudio	£15	£500–600	£300–450
Microphones	£3–5	£15+	£10+
Mixer (16 inputs/ 4 outputs)	£10–30	£500+	£500+
PA System (6–800 watts; 2x speakers; power amp; multicore and stage box)	£40	£2500+	£2000+

Insurance

Once you've bought all this expensive gear you'll need to insure it. It might seem like money down the drain, until you discover the van window broken and your favourite amp missing! Take some care when you sort out your insurance. It's worth shopping around to get the best deal. Some companies specialise in musical instrument insurance; for example, one charges £4–5 per year for each hundred pounds worth of gear.

Getting in Touch

National Organizations:

Arts Council of Great Britain
105 Piccadilly, London W1
Telephone: 01·629 9495
**National Association of
Arts Centres**
The Secretary
Washington Arts Centre
Biddick Farm, Fatfield, Washington
Tyne and Wear NE38 8AB
Telephone: 01·416 6440
Will provide information on your
nearest arts centre (there are
300 around the country). The
centres vary considerably but
some have a lot of equipment,
venues etc. and do workshops.
Musicians' Union
(National Office)
60–62 Clapham Road, London SW9
Telephone: 01·582 5566
**British Music
Information Centre**
10 Stratford Place, London W1
Telephone: 01·499 8567
**Independent Labels
Association (ILA)**
56 Wigmore Street, London W1
Telephone: 01·935 2303
**Customer Services
Advisor of MCPR**
(Mechanical Copyright and
Protection Society)
Elgar House
41 Streatham High Road
London SW16
Telephone: 01·769 4400
**Inter-Action Social Enterprise
Trust Limited**
Royal Victoria Dock, London E16 1BT
Telephone: 01 511 0411
Can provide training and
consultancy on setting up and
running projects

Regional Organizations
London:

Lewisham Academy of Music
77 Watson Street, Deptford SE8
Telephone: 01·691 0307
Provides individual and class
tuition. Good contact point.
Islington Arts Factory
2 Parkhurst Road, London N7
Telephone: 01·607 0561
Has two rehearsal studios for
hire by the hour, one fully
equipped. The music officer helps
arrange gigs, demo tapes etc.
Also does keyboard workshops.
**Cockpit Theatre and Arts
Workshop**
Gateforth Street, London NW8
Telephone: 01·262 7907
Recording studio, music workshop.
The Basement Project (C.L.Y.P)
29 Shelton Street, London WC2
Telephone: 01·240 8377
Recording studio, other
musicians etc. Can go
individually or as a band.
Islington Bus Company
Community Resource Centre
Palmer Place, London N7
Telephone: 01·609 0226
Inter-Action Centre Limited
15 Wilkin Street, London NW5 3NG
Telephone: 01·267 9421
Rehearsal space/equipment for
hire/recording facilities
WAC – Weekend Arts College
c/o Inter-Action
15 Wilkin Street. London NW5 3NG
Telephone: 01·267 9421
Jazz Centre Society
35 Great Russell Street
London WC1
Telephone: 01·204 2430
Can also put people in touch
with jazz centres and musicians'
collectives nationwide.
Lambeth Adult Education Institute
Brixton Centre
130 Ferndale Road, London SW4
Telephone: 01·737 1234
They do a course called
"Music Biz" which they are
including in their next
programme beginning September
1984 (Mon. and Wed. 7–9 p.m.)
**Chelsea and Westminster
Adult Education Institute**
Marlborough School

Sloane Avenue, Chelsea
London SW3
Telephone: 01·589 2044
They have a course in rock guitar;
pop keyboard; pop and rock style
singing (which includes how to
use a recording studio); pop
song-writing workshop. They also
have an occasional 10-week course
called "Pop Music from the
Business Angle" for details
Telephone: 01·828 9614

Midlands:

West Bromwich College of Commerce and Technology
Woden Road South, Wednesbury
West Midlands
Telephone: 021·569 4590
Does courses and has a 4-track
recording studio.

Northampton Collective
Secretary
74 Delapre Street
Northampton NN4 9HA
Telephone: 0604 61665
Provides other musicians,
advice etc.

The Clock House
University of Keele
Keele, Staffordshire
Telephone: 0782 621111
Has electronic music facilities
and recording studio.

Triangle Arts Centre
Gosta Green, Birmingham
Telephone: 021·359 3979
Has a recording studio and does
music workshops. Ask for the
music officer.

Jazz Central
184 Corporation Street
Birmingham B4 6QB
Telephone: 021·236 4379

Saltley Music Workshop
9–11 Washwood Heath Road
Saltley, Birmingham 8
Telephone: 021·328 1954
Have set up a music
co-operative which helps
with gigs and provides tuition,
contacts etc.

Coventry Education Department
Council House, Earl Street
Coventry CB1 5RR
Telephone: 0203 25555
Equipment and touring workshops.

North East:

Riverside Music Co-op
Project North East
5 Saville Place
Newcastle-upon-Tyne
Telephone: 0632 617856
Provides rehearsal space,
equipment. A building complex is
in process of completion.

Gateshead Musicians' Collective
North East Work Trust
28 Mosley Street
Newcastle
Tel: (ex-directory)

North West:

Jazz Centre North
Band on the Wall, Swan Street
Manchester 1
Telephone: 061·834 5109
Good contact point. Provides
lists and information and has
live local bands six
nights a week.

The Arts Centre
Wirral College of Art and
Design and Adult Studies
Whetstone Lane, Birkenhead
Merseyside L42 2SW
Telephone: 051·647 9059
Is chiefly concerned with young
people; wide range of facilities,
tuition and equipment. Includes
electronic music, workshop,
percussion room etc.

The Great George's Project
Great George's Street
Liverpool 1
Telephone: 051·709 5109
Provides free rehearsal space.
Some instruments; lots of sound
equipment (two ¼ inch
semi-professional sound).

North:

Darlington Arts Centre
Vain Terrace, Darlington, DL3 7AX
Telephone: 0325 483271
They have local gigs in their
bar and theatre every two weeks.
Also "The Music Cellar"
for rehearsals.

Brewery Arts Centre
Highgate, Kendal, Cumbria
Telephone: 0539 25133
This is a good information
contact point. Also has a venue
and theatre seating for 250.

Dovecot Arts Centre
Dovecot Street, Stockton-on-Tees
Cleveland TS18 1LL
Telephone: 0642 611625/61659
Has rehearsal space; courses
in jazz-rock; a venue for
local bands; PA system and
lighting rig.

Sunderland Musicians' Collective
c/o The Bunker, 29 Stockton Road
Sunderland
Telephone: 0783 654948

**Sunderland Youth
Employment Project**
29 Stockton Road
Sunderland SR1 7AQ
Telephone: 0783 40661

Consett Music Project
c/o John Kearney
The Old Miners' Hall
Percy Terrace, Delves Lane
Consett, Co. Durham
Telephone: 0207 507310

Durham Music
c/o Keith Naisbett, Fowlers Yard
Back Silver St., Durham City
Telephone: 0385 69576

**Middlesbrough Musicians'
Collective**
c/o Steve Graham
44 Kinloch Road
Normanby, Middlesbrough
Cleveland TS6 0ES
Telephone: 0642 452843
To meet other musicians; help,
advice etc.

Riverside Music
c/o Keith Jeffrey, 31 High View
Wallsend,
Tyne and Wear NE28 8SR
Telephone: 091 626922

Sunderland Musicians' Collective
The Bunker, 29 Stockton Road
Sunderland
Telephone: 0783 650020

Unemployed Musicians' Studio
c/o Peter Gowland
Unemployment Field Office
St John's Church, Park Road
Hartlepool, Cleveland
Telephone: 0429 67457

Whitehaven Musicians' Collective
c/o Bridget Roberts
Howgill Centre
Howgill St, Whitehaven, Cumbria
(No telephone)

Eastern:

Colchester Arts Centre
St Mary-at-the-Wall
Church Street
Colchester CO1 1NF
Telephone: 0206 577301
Provides facilities for gigs,
mostly for local bands. Also has
an alternative cabaret; jazz
workshop including tuition and
instruments; rock workshop. Very
strong folk contingent
(have recorded own albums etc.).

Eastern Jazz Federation
c/o Eastern Arts
8–9 Bridge Street, Cambridge
Telephone: 0223 357596

Backs Record Distribution
Saint Mary's Works
St Mary's Plain, Norwich
Telephone: 0603 26221
For information on venues,
rehearsal space, contacts etc.
in East Anglia.

South West:

South-West Jazz
Exeter and Devon Arts Centre
Bradninch Place, Gandy Street
Exeter EX4 3LS
Telephone: 0392 218368

Plymouth Arts Centre
38 Looe St, Plymouth
Telephone: 0752 28072/660060
The film officer there is running
a video music development

project with a team of experienced musicians going out to youth groups and schools. Individual enquiries welcome to the film officer.

Cornwall Youth Jazz Orchestra
c/o Leslie Brixton
8 Palace Road
St Austell, Cornwall PL25 4OE
(No telephone)

Devon Youth Jazz Orchestra
c/o Alan Hayden
West Devon Area Education Office
Civic Centre, Plymouth
Devon PL1 2EW
Telephone: 0752 21312

Gloucestershire Youth Jazz Orchestra
c/o The White House
277 Bristol Road, Quedgeley
Gloucestershire GL2 6QP
(No telephone)

South:

Jazz South
13 Hartington Road, Brighton
East Sussex
Telephone: 0273 672242
Deals with jazz, rock, funk etc.

Scotland:

Scottish Arts Council
19 Charlotte Square
Edinburgh EHZ 4DF
Telephone: 031·226 6051

Platform
5 Buccleuch Street, Edinburgh
Telephone: 031·226 4179

Wales:

Welsh Arts Council
Holst House, Museum Place
Cardiff CF1 3NX
Telephone: 0222 394711

West Wales Association for the Arts
Dark Gate, 3 Red Street
Carmarthen, Dyfed SA 31 12L
Telephone: 0267 394711

Aberystwyth Arts Centre:
Penglais, Aberystwyth
Dyfed SY 23 DF.

Telephone: 0970 4277
Studio space and venue.

Chapter Cardiff's Workshops and Centre for the Arts
Canton, Cardiff CF5 1QE
Telephone: 0222 396061
Has a local band playing in the bar each night. Good for information on equipment hire, contacts, space etc.

City Centre Youth Project
58 Charles Street, Cardiff
Telephone: 0222 31700
Have equipped rehearsal studios. Do formal tuition and jamming sessions. Local bands regularly get together. They're hoping to build a recording studio as soon as they raise the money. Mainly for unemployed 16–24 year olds.

Black Bands:

Minority Arts Advisory Service (MAAS)
Beauchamp Lodge
2 Warwick Crescent, London W2
Telephone: 01·286 1854
Has a training officer who will deal with questions and give advice when able. They also have regional offices.

Brent Black Music Co-op
86 Hugh Gaitskell House
Butler Road, London NW10
Telephone: 01·568 0678

Simba Project
42–45 Artillery Place
London SE18
Telephone: 01·317 0451
Gives music workshops, have recording studio, do tapes and professional recordings.

Jenako Arts
49 Balls Pond Road, London N1
Telephone: 01·249 6062

Women's Bands:

The West London Women's Music Project
Based in Acton
Telephone: 01·221 0534
               01·740 9285 –

Hold jam sessions in the evening;
provide rehearsal space,
equipment, instruments and
amplification. Have small P.A.
system, bass and guitar combo,
guitar and drum kits and
percussion available for use.
Hope to have recording
facilities soon.

Women's Musicians' Collective
Shelf 13, 73 Walmgate, York
(No telephone)

Women's Revolutions Per Minute
62 Woodstock Road
Birmingham B13 9BN
Telephone: 021·449 7041
Provides advice, contacts,
reference point etc.
Available day and night.

**There is now a women's music
magazine called:**
Woman Sound
It's available from:
Unit N/O, Studio 411
Metropolitan Wharf, Wapping Wall
London E1
(No telephone)

Try these groups
in your area:

■ Contact your Regional Arts
Association and ask for the Music
Officer who should be able to
provide information about local
collectives, venues and possible
sources of finance – even though
they don't deal primarily with
rock and pop. They'll also be
able to put you in contact with
your nearest community arts group
or arts centre.
■ Try your local County Council,
Department of Education. They'll
have a Music Advisor, Officer or
Centre. Though mostly
concerned with schools,
they can be useful sources of
local advice, e.g.
■ The ILEA Music Centre
Telephone: 01·821 8011
■ Your local Citizens Advice Bureau
(number in the phone-book).
■ Musicians Union –

Regional Officers (see under
'National' for the
central office):

Scotland:
35 Wellington Street, Glasgow C2
Telephone: 041·248 3723

North-West:
4 Roby Street, Manchester 1 3AG
Telephone: 061·236 1764

Midlands/East/North-East:
14–16 Bristol Street
Birmingham B5 7AA
Telephone: 021·622 3870

North/North-East:
c/o J. Jenkins
135 Wellington St, Glasgow
Telephone: 041·248 3723

South-East:
60/62 Clapham Road, London
Telephone: 01·582 5566

South-West:
1 New Road, Trull, Taunton
Telephone: 0823 8257

■ Colleges of Further Education
and Technical Colleges will offer
tuition and perhaps space.

Rotary Clubs
Rotary International in
Great Britain and N. Ireland
Sheen Lane House
Sheen Lane, London SW14
Telephone: 01·878 0931
■ Your local Youth Training
Centre or Youth Community Centre.
Some of these will have
noticeboards where you can make
contact with other
young musicians.
■ Remember to check your local
record shop who will have
information about any local
independent record companies.
It's well worth checking up on
these as they are starting up
all over the place.
■ Remember that your local
Regional Arts Association can
put you in contact with your
nearest community arts group or
arts centre.

Getting Going

In order to get your Breaks Centre going, you need as much help as you can get. This section of the book gives you ideas on where you can go for information and advice, and lists lots of useful addresses. Remember, you can lose nothing by asking – and you never know what you will gain!

Kick-off

In order to track down specialist advice and information on what kind of help is available locally, start off with the following:

Your local library

The reference library is your best bet. Some libraries provide special services for local small enterprises, and a lot of the help they have to offer will be relevant to your Breaks Centre.

Citizen's Advice Bureau

You'll find the number in the phone book. They can offer a very wide range of services, from legal advice to photocopying! They'll be able to help you get in touch with other organizations in your area.

Your Local Council

You may need to contact any of these departments within your Council:

- Economic Development Unit
- Employment Development Unit
- Co-operative Development Agency
- Valuer's Department
- Architect's Department
- Education Department

Phone up and explain what you need to know and you'll be put through to the right person.

Enterprise Agencies

These operate in local areas and are there to help small businesses or people who want to start one. However, they should be a good source of help on the business side of your Breaks Centre. Check with your Council or try the Community pages in the Thomsons Directory. Otherwise, phone Business in the Community (see page 120) – the umbrella organization that deals with Enterprise Agencies to find out where the nearest one is.

Small Firms Service

Run by the government, they have a free telephone advice service which can answer many specific queries. They also have experienced counsellors who may be able to help you.

Phone the operator and ask for Freephone 2444 to get in touch.

COSIRA

(The Council of Small Industries in Rural Areas).

Another government-run advice service which covers rural areas only. Any of the above organizations will be able to tell you if COSIRA covers your area.

Getting advice:

There are lots of organizations that can offer all kinds of advice and professional expertise. These are some of the most important:

Manpower Services Commission (MSC)

Moorfoot, Sheffield S1 4PQ
Telephone: 0742 753275
Responsible for all government courses and training schemes. There are regional offices throughout the country.
Also funds some schemes (see under Grants/Aid)

Local Authorities

They usually have an Economic or Industrial Development Unit which will provide contacts and information.

Business in the Community

227A City Road, London EC1

Telephone: 01 · 253 3716
A consortium which helps the
creation and expansion of small
enterprises.

Practical Action
Victoria Chambers
16–20 Strutton Ground
London SW1P 2HP
Telephone: 01 · 222 3341/2
A Youth Enterprise Scheme to
assist young people who are
setting up their own enterprises.

Livewire Scheme
Shell (UK) Ltd
Shell-Mex House, The Strand
London WC2
Telephone: 01 · 257 3000

National Extension College
18 Brookland Avenue
Cambridge CB2 2HN
Telephone: 0223 31664
Help for young people who want to
raise money and start up
business ventures.

Young Enterprise
48 Bryanston Square
London W1
Telephone: 01 · 262 6367

**Inter-Action Social Enterprise
Trust**
Occupation Preparation Systems
Royal Victoria Dock London E16 1BT
Telephone: 01 511 0411

Project North-East
5 Saville Place
Newcastle-Upon-Tyne
NW1 8OU
Telephone: 0632 617856
Helps development of employment
ideas in N.E. Runs IT Centre and
Newcastle Youth Centre for
Enterprises.

North Lewisham Law Centre
Telephone: 01 · 692 5355
Deals specifically with the legal
problems of young people.

Reach
1st Floor, Victoria House
Southampton Row, London WC1 4DH
Telephone: 01 · 404 0940
They place retired executives
from the business
world in charitable organizations
and may be able to provide youth with

advisers or other expertise.

Setting up as a Co-operative:

**Co-operative
Development Agency**
20 Albert Embankment
London SE1
Telephone: 01 · 211 4633
Or phone 01 · 211 3351 for
information on your
nearest CDA.
Provides help, information and
advice on all
areas of starting
up and running a co-operative.

Co-operative Union
Holyoake House
1 Hanover Street
Manchester M60 0AS
Telephone: 061 · 832 4300
National advisory and information
organization. Runs full and part
time courses in business practice
for young people between
15 and 19.
Can assist new co-operatives with
legal and constitutional
questions, taxation etc.

**Industrial Common
Ownership Movement**
7 Corn Exchange, Leeds LS1 7BP
Telephone: 0532 461737/8

Co-operative Bank plc
(Small Businesses & Co-ops)
Business Development Manager
Head Office, PO Box 101
1 Balloon Street
Manchester M60 4EP
Telephone: 061 · 832 3456
Ext 280/282
Very involved with worker co-ops.
Help and advice available at the
Head Office special unit. Enquiries
are welcome at all branches and
they provide wide-ranging general
and specialist financial services
for worker co-ops.

Co-operative Research Unit
Faculty of Technology
The Open University
Walton Hall, Milton Keynes MK7 6AA
Telephone: 0908 653303

Job Ownership Ltd (JOL)
9 Poland Street, London W1V 3DG
Telephone: 01·437 5511
"An independent non-profit making
consultancy unit for the
promotion of worker ownership".
Advice, information etc.

Instant Muscle
c/o Rank Xerox (UK) Ltd
Cambridge House
Oxford Road, Middx. UB8 1HS
Telephone: 0895 51166
They run odd-jobs co-operatives
for young people and can advise
you on how to start your own.

Courses and Training:

Nowadays there are literally
hundreds of courses run by all
sorts of organizations – from
Unemployment Action Centres to
Community Centres. Many of these
are free, and could be useful
to you. For music tuition, ask at
your local Adult Education
Centre, College of Further
Education or Education Department
at the town Council. If what you
want isn't available, try
advertising on noticeboards at
your Community Centre or Arts
Centre, in shop windows and at your
local music shop. There's growing
interest in special courses for the
rock and pop world. There are some
starting up in London:

**Lambeth Adult
Education Centre**
Brixton Centre, Ferndale Road
London SW4
Telephone: 01·737 1234
do a course called "Music Biz".

**Chelsea and Westminster
Adult Education Institute**
Marlborough School
Sloane Avenue, Chelsea
London SW3
are holding a number of pop/rock
classes and also a course called
"Pop Music from the Business Angle".
See Getting In Touch (page 00)
for more organizations to
contact.

If you want to learn more about
the business and financial side
of your Breaks Centre, there are
lots of opportunities via local
colleges and government-sponsored
training – especially if you are
unemployed. Ask at your local Job
Centre for further information.

Your Breaks Centre and the Dole:

To get supplementary benefit
(from the DHSS) or unemployment
benefit (from the Department of
Employment), you must be
available for work. Your benefit
may therefore stop if you get
involved in any kind of activity
which you can't drop straightaway
to go for a job or an activity.
If you're claiming benefit and
getting involved in setting up a
Breaks Centre, this isn't likely
to be a problem since your
meetings and rehearsals will
happen at all sorts of times and
you'll be in a position to
arrange them.
If you're on supplementary
benefit, you'll normally be able
to earn up to £4 per week without
your benefit being affected.
However, any money that you earn
for yourself – rather than for
the Breaks Centre – above that
level, will be deducted from your
girocheque: *AND NO MATTER
HOW LITTLE MONEY YOU EARN
ON ANY ONE DAY, YOU MUST
ALWAYS REPORT IT TO YOUR
SOCIAL SECURITY OFFICE.*
If your Breaks Centre really
looks like taking off and you're
thinking about going into it as a
full-time venture, you may be
eligible for the Manpower
Services Commission's Enterprise
Allowance Scheme. Normally,
unemployed people who decide to
set up their own business or
small enterprise full-time, will
lose their benefit. However, if
you're accepted on to the

Enterprise Allowance Scheme, you'll be paid £40 per week for up to 62 weeks to supplement the income of your Breaks Centre while it's getting established. There are a number of conditions you have to fulfil before you can become eligible for the scheme: most importantly, you have to be over 18, have £1,000 to invest, and your Centre must be approved as a business proposition by the MSC. You can go in as a co-operative, in which case not less than half the members must be on the Scheme. If you're interested in setting up your Breaks Centre as a commercial proposition – and remember, it's a big step – contact your Job Centre for further information.

Getting Backing

There are four main sources of financial backing for your Breaks Centre:
■ Fundraising events
■ Firms, trusts and charities
■ Local government
■ Individuals and private organizations
This section will give you a few more ideas about raising money; it also lists some useful names and addresses.

1. Fundraising Events
The possibilities are endless! Some of the things you might consider are – odd jobs, social evenings, sponsored events and collecting items to exchange for cash.
There's a useful collection of fundraising ideas published by The Scout Association (Baden Powell House, Queens Gate, London WC2A 1JB) called *Fund Raising – A Collection of Ideas.*

2. Firms, Trusts and Charities
When looking around for organizations to approach, pick your list carefully. Charities and Trusts have rules about who and what they will give money to. The Charities Aid Foundation publishes a very useful book, *The Directory of Grant Making Trusts,* a guide to thousands of organizations which give money to different groups. They've also produced a book called *Presenting Your Case.*
You can make a list of likely firms to approach in your area by looking in the local paper – ads as well as news items – checking the Yellow Pages and contacting your local Chamber of Commerce.
Other possible sources of money are organizations like the Lions Clubs, Rotary, and Round Table which raise money for charitable and community causes. To contact the branches near you, ask at the library or Citizen's Advice Bureau.

3. Local Government
Getting money out of "the Government" can sound very difficult and complicated. Well, it's not! Your Local Authority is the branch of government most likely to give you money. It must spend its money for the benefit of people living locally and it funds local groups and projects in the same way.
When you apply to your Local Authority for funds, you'll probably do it with the help of a friendly local councillor, youth worker or adviser, but there are some important things to keep in mind even before you fill in the application form.
■ Decisions on grants are taken by local councillors so it's important to use any opportunity you get – like your public meetings – to get to know the key councillors, and if possible to get the support of one or two of them.
■ Many Local Authorities employ staff to work specifically on funding local projects. Their titles vary, but they are usually called something like "community development officers". They are there to provide advice and to help you with your application. Phone your local Council and explain who you want to contact and they'll

put you in touch with the right person.
■ Remember, even if your Local Authority can't give you money, it can provide loans, premises, even supplies – so keep on pushing!
There's a useful book, edited by Michael Norton called *Raising Money from Government* (Directory of Social Change, 9 Mansfield Place, London NW3 1HS) which will give you more information.

4. Individuals and Private Organizations

Approaching individuals in your area will be largely a question of getting to know the individuals in your community who are likely to donate funds – and, of course, using local publicity as much as possible in order to get yourselves known by them! As in all applications for funding, pay attention to the presentation and pick your targets with care.

There are a number of books which cover the whole area of how to raise funds, all of which you should be able to get through your local library. One of the most useful, which you might like to have on hand, is *Money Raising A–Z*, National Association of Youth Clubs (1977), PO Box 1, Nuneaton, Warwickshire CV11 4DB.

Sample Constitution

For a Breaks for young bands association or centre

Name

1. The name of the association shall be

Objects

2. The objects of the Association shall be:
(a) To promote the benefit of the young people and other inhabitants of_____

without distinction to sex or of political, religious or other opinions by associating the local authorities, voluntary organization, young people and other inhabitants in a common effort to advance education and to provide facilities in the interests of social welfare for recreation and leisure-time occupation with the object of improving the conditions of life for the young people and other inhabitants of

(b) To establish or to secure the use or establishment of a music and arts centre and to maintain and manage, or to co-operate with any voluntary body or statutory authority in the maintenance and management of such a Centre for activities promoted by the Association and its constituent bodies in furtherance of the above objects.

Powers

3. To further these objects but not otherwise, the Association may:
(a) Arrange and provide for, or join in arranging and providing for, the holding of concerts, exhibitions, meetings, lectures, classes, workshops and training courses, and other leisure-time activities.
(b) Cause to be written and to print, publish, issue and circulate either free of charge or otherwise such papers, books, periodicals, pamphlets or other documents, films, computer discs, records or recorded tapes (audio and video) as shall further the objects.
(c) Purchase, take on lease, licence or in exchange, hire or otherwise acquire any property and any rights and privileges necessary for the promotion of the objects and construct, maintain and alter any buildings or structures necessary for the work of the Association.
(d) Subject to such consents as may be required by law, to sell, let, license, mortgage, dispose of or turn to account all or any of the property or assets of the Association.

(e) Raise funds and invite and receive contributions from any person or body whatsoever by way of subscriptions and otherwise provided that the Association shall not undertake any permanent trading activities in raising funds for its primary charitable objects.

(f) Receive money on deposit or loan and borrow or raise and invest money in such a manner as the Association shall think fit subject to such consents as required by law.

Membership

4. Membership of the Association shall be open to young people between the ages of _____ and _____ residing in _____

_____

who support the objects of the Association. There will be three types of membership: (1) individual; (2) group; (3) associate. There shall be no age or geographical limit to associate membership.

Subscription

5. The Committee shall set the annual subscription for each type of member, and may set any and all other charges and fees.

Management committee

6. (a) The conduct of policy, finance and the day-to-day running of the affairs of the Association shall be controlled by a Management Committee.

(b) The Committee shall consist of not less than _____ members elected annually by ballot at the Annual General meeting or at a Special Meeting called for the purpose of replacing vacancies on the Committee. Only those members with membership of at least _____ weeks shall be allowed voting rights or to hold any office, except at the meeting to adopt this Constitution. At that meeting, every individual attending who meets the membership requirements will have one vote.

(c) The Committee shall appoint a Chairperson, Secretary and

Treasurer and such other officers as they may deem necessary.

(d) The Committee shall meet regularly, but at least twelve times a year.

(e) The Committee shall have power to co-opt as additional members such persons as, in their opinion, are able to render special service, so long as these are no more in number than half the total number of elected Committee members.

(f) The duties of the Committee shall be to safeguard the interests of members by providing or securing the premises, equipment, leadership, staff and finance to the best of their abilities, and by encouraging members to take a full and active part in the running of the Association.

(g) The Committee shall have the right for good and sufficient reason to suspend or to terminate the membership of an individual or an affiliated group. The individual member or the individual representing the affiliated group shall have the right to be heard by the Committee before the final decision is made.

(h) Nominations for election to the Committee shall be submitted in writing, countersigned by the person nominated, not less than seven days before the Annual General Meeting, except for the first meeting which adopts the Constitution.

(i) The quorum for this Committee shall be at least half of the elected members.

(j) Members of the Committee who fail to attend _____ meetings in succession without tendering apologies will be deemed to have resigned.

Accounts and minutes

7. The Committee shall cause the Treasurer to keep proper accounts of all monies belonging to the Association. The Committee shall cause a minute book to be kept by the Association. The Committee and any sub-committees shall enter a record of all proceedings and resolutions in this book. This will be presented regularly to the members and at least once a year to a General Meeting of the Association.

Annual and special general meetings

8. (a) Annual Meetings shall be held within fifteen months of the previous meeting. Not less than twenty-one days' notice of the meeting shall be given. Any person wishing to submit any matter for discussion shall give not less than seven days' notice to the member of the Management Committee nominated for this task. Those entitled to vote shall be those present at the meeting who are members as defined in clause 4.

(b) Special General Meetings may be convened at any time by the Committee and shall be convened by them on receipt of a request signed by_____ members.

(c) The quorum required for the Annual General Meeting and Special General Meeting is ten per cent of the membership and fifty per cent of the Committee.

Voting

9. Except for amendments to this Constitution all questions arising at any meeting shall be decided by a simple majority of those present and entitled to vote. No member shall have more than one vote. In case of an equality of votes the Chairperson shall have a second or casting vote.

Amendments

10. The above Constitution shall only be altered by resolution passed by a two-thirds majority of the members at a General Meeting. Notice of proposed amendments to the Constitution must be given in writing not less than twentyone days before the General Meeting. No change shall be made to this Constitution which shall cause the Association to cease to be a charity by law.

House rules

11. The Committee shall have the power to adopt and issue bye-laws and/or house rules. These bye-laws and house rules shall come into operation immediately, provided always that they shall be subject to review by the Association at General Meetings. They shall not be inconsistent with the provisions of this Constitution.

Finance

12. (a) All money raised by or on behalf of the Association shall be applied to further the objects of the Association and for no other purpose. Nothing contained in this Constitution shall prevent the payment in good faith of reasonable and proper payment to any employee of the Association or the repayment of reasonable out-of-pocket expenses.

(b) The accounts shall be audited at least once a year by the auditor or auditors appointed at the Annual General Meeting.

(c) An audited statement of accounts for the last financial year shall be submitted by the Committee to the Annual General Meeting.

(d) A bank account shall be opened in the name of the Association with _____

_____

Bank Ltd., of _____

_____

or with such other bank as the Committee shall from time to time decide. The Committee shall authorize in writing the Treasurer, the Secretary of the Association and two members of the Committee to sign cheques on behalf of the Association. All cheques must be signed by not less than two of the four authorized signatories.

Dissolution

13. In the event of the Association being dissolved any property remaining after satisfaction of all its debts shall be put at the disposal of

_____

_____ or to some other charitable purpose, so long as no individual member or group of members shall take any share of such disposal.

This Constitution was adopted as the Constitution of the _____ Breaks for Young Bands Association at a Public Meeting at_____

_____

on _____ 19

Signed

Chairperson_____

Witness_____

More Reading

Books:

How to Succeed in the Music Business
Alan Dann and John Underwood
Wise Publications
Lots of advice, plus useful names and addresses.

Working in the World of Music
Julia M. Parker and Anna Alston
Batsford Academic and Educational Ltd.

The Rock Music Source Book
Bob Macken, Peter Fornatale and Bill Ayres
Doubleday Anchor Books.

The Rock Yearbook
ed. Al Clark, Virgin Books
Contains reference section on record companies, recording studios etc.

The Illustrated Encyclopaedia of Black Music
Salamander Books Ltd.

Woman Sound
Unit N10, Studio 411
Metropolitan Wharf
Wapping Wall, London E1
A new journal specially for women's bands.

Studio Recording for Musicians
Fred Miller
Consolidated Music Publishers
New York
An in-depth guide that takes you from basic recording equipment and procedures to mixing and mastering techniques.

Rock Hardware: the Instruments, Equipment and Technology of Rock
ed. Tony Bacon
Blandford Press UK

Home Recording for Musicians
Craig Anderton
Guitar Player Books
New York
All the information you need to make professional-quality recordings at home. Covers tape-decks, mikes, mixing, audio equipment etc.

Studio Test Guide
International Musician and Recording World
Circulation Dept
The Northern and Shell Building
PO Box 381
Mill Harbour, London E14 9TW
A comprehensive guide to professional and home recording equipment, plus a directory of studios all over the country.

On The Road Guide '84
International Musician and Recording World
(as above)
Includes information about venues, PA and lighting hire, truck hire, local music shops, 24-hour garages etc.

Sound Reinforcement Guide
International Musician and Recording World
(as above)
Directory of compact and backline amps, PA systems, mixing desks, stage microphones and accessories.

What Keyboard
Monthly from newsagents or direct from International Musician and Recording World.

Electronic Soundmaker and Computer Music
Monthly from newsagents or direct from International Musician and Recording World.

The White Book
(The White Book)
The Old House
Shepperton Studios Centre
Studios Road, Shepperton
Middx TW17 0QJ
This useful reference book and the

one below list names and addresses of promoters, venues, hire companies, record companies etc:

"The Music Week Directory"
Music Week Publications
40 Long Acre
London WC2E 9J2
Directory of Arts Centres
Arts Council of GB in association with John Offord (Publications) Ltd
Will tell you of your nearest centre and its facilities.
Small Scale Touring Venues
An Arts Council Publication.
Floodlight
Inner London Education Authority
Lists music courses,
London-wide.

Magazines

Music UK
Folly Publications
26-28 Addison Road
Bromley, Kent
International Musician and Recording World
Cover Publications Ltd
Northern and Shell Building
PO Box 381
Mill Harbour, London E14 9TW
Beat Instrumental
113 Parkfield Street
London N1
Black Beat International
143 Mare Street
Hackney, London E8 3RH
Black Echoes
113 Parkfield Street
London N1
Blues and Soul
42 Hanway Street, London W1
Sound International
Link House Group
Dingwall Avenue, Croydon
Record Business
Hyde House
13 Langley Street, London WC2
Black Music and Jazz Reviews
153 Praed Street, London WC2
Melody Maker
24/34 Meymott Street, London SE1
Zigzag
Talbot Road, London W11

NME
(New Musical Express)
5-7 Carnaby Street, London W1
Record Mirror
40 Long Acre, London WC2E 9JT
Jamming
45-53 Sinclair Road, London W14
Echoes
Rococo House, 238 City Road
London EC1 1LA
The Wire
72 Farm Lane, Fulham, London SW6
Jazz Express
29 Romilly Street, London W1

About the Authors

ED Berman:

ED Berman MBE is the founder of Inter-Action Trust, its centres in Kentish Town, the London Docklands and its various associated charities, trusts and companies. He is a Harvard Graduate and Rhodes Scholar to Oxford. His many other roles include: playwright, animateur/community artist, educational film-maker, theatre producer and director. At the beginning of the Seventies, the Council of Europe described ED Berman as 'the most dynamic phenomenon on the British Community Arts scene'. At the end of the Seventies, a *Newsweek Magazine* feature summarized him as 'one of the most remarkable figures in world theatre . . . a unique blend of artist and activist'.

ED Berman acquired dual citizenship (UK–USA) when he became a British Subject in 1976. From 1977, he has been developing a method called MIY – Make It Yourself which enables young people to set up and run their own projects and co-operatives. Dozens of groups have produced their own singles and LPs using this approach. He has also helped set up various kinds of recording projects for young people around the country.

He was awarded an MBE in 1979 for services to arts and the community. In 1982–83, he was Special Adviser to the Secretary of State for the Environment on Inner City Matters with particular reference to the voluntary sector.

Berman is currently the Chief Executive of the Inter-Action Social Enterprise Trust which runs Community Computers, Youth Options, OPS-Occupation Preparation Systems and the Inter-Action Training Institute. This charity also helps voluntary agencies set up creative projects in their own communities.

Mike Jay:

Mike Jay is an independent film-maker who has specialized in working with rock bands. He began directing in Berlin in 1981–2, when he made videos for a number of West and East German bands which were shown on TV in Germany, Poland and Russia. Returning to London in 1982, he began directing videos for English bands, and his work has appeared on 'Top of the Pops' and 'Saturday Superstore' as well as on cable TV in the USA and Japan. In addition to working on this book, his writing includes a documentary series and a horror film.

Mike Lambert:

Mike Lambert is a Film Assistant at the BBC and a freelance music journalist, contributing to various magazines and to BBC Radio London's rock show 'Breakthrough' – the longest established show of its kind on local radio in the country. He has a particular interest in the newer bands on the circuit. Out of this have come many features on these bands, and he's kept in contact through the good and the bad times. Much of the experience he's gained from these bands and their promoters, record companies, pluggers and managers is distilled into this book.

About Inter-Action

Inter-Action Trust is a national educational charity founded in 1968 by ED Berman MBE. Inter-Action has been described by the Council of Europe as "The most exciting community development agency in Europe." Summarising his impressions about Inter-Action, HRH Prince Charles said " . . . these imaginative and refreshingly simple schemes are exactly the sort of thing we aim to encourage . . . "

Inter-Action's operating company is Inter-Action Social Enterprise Trust Ltd. This charitable company pioneers new services and projects for the voluntary and statutory sectors. It helps others establish new projects for community benefit and new companies for job creation purposes.

Social enterprise is the application of creativity, initiative-taking, leadership and management skills for social benefit.

The Centre for Social Enterprise runs training courses and provides consultancy in the UK and abroad. The areas these cover are management and enterprise skills, group work and the social, educational and participatory use of arts, the media and creativity techniques. It also develops new materials and model projects.

Examples of this approach are: Community Computers – an advisory service and resource unit for voluntary and statutory sector agencies. One of its main activities is helping others set up Community Computer Camps. It also runs consultancy sessions for agencies wishing to computerise.

Youth Options Menu – a DES funded experimental project helping youth agencies extend their work, particularly with the young unemployed, by sharing good practice and pooling resources.

Inter-Action has also developed OPS – Occupational Preparation Systems for the training and assessment of young unemployed people. These are exciting hands-on programmed learning materials in slide-tape or computer formats. Some of the systems guide young people and their teachers or trainers through planned, practical, real experiences of job finding and community exploration.

One OPS system, MIY (Make-It-Yourself), was developed with youth groups over a 5 year period. MIY takes young people through the practical experience of setting up and running a trial co-operative enterprise.

For more information contact –
Inter-Action Social Enterprise Trust
Royal Victoria Dock, London E16 1BT
Telephone: 01 511 0411

Inter-Action also produces a wide range of
similar publications for practical projects and
training. OPS – Occupation Preparation Systems, a
branch of Inter-Action, produces hands-on training modules.
Further information from:
Inter-Action In-Print
Royal Victoria Dock
London E16 1BT
01-511 0411

Printed by Thetford Press Limited, Thetford and London